THE OTHER SIDE

OF PROFIT

Edited by

LLOYD L. BYARS, Ph. D.

Associate Professor of Management
The School of Business Administration
Georgia State University
Atlanta, Georgia

and

MICHAEL H. MESCON, Ph. D.

Chairman, Department of Management
The School of Business Administration
Georgia State University
Atlanta, Georgia

 W. B. SAUNDERS COMPANY
PHILADELPHIA LONDON TORONTO

W. B. Saunders Company: West Washington Square
Philadelphia, Pa. 19105

12 Dyott Street
London, WC1A 1DB

833 Oxford Street
Toronto, Ontario M8Z 5T9, Canada

Library of Congress Cataloging in Publication Data

Byars, Lloyd L

The other side of profit.

1. Industry — Social aspects — United States — Addresses,
essays, lectures.   I. Mescon, Michael H., joint author.
II. Title.

HD60.5.U5B93   658.4'08   74–17750
ISBN 0–7216–2245–3

The Other Side of Profit   ISBN 0–7216–2245–3

Last digit is the print number: 9   8   7   6   5   4   3   2   1

To our wives—LINDA and ENID

Preface

In recent years, business and businessmen have once again discovered the true meaning of scapegoat. Under attack is the private enterprise system and especially its key component—profit. Admittedly, business has its seamy side, but so do religion, education, law, medicine, and labor, to cite just a few. While some businessmen are corrupt, they certainly don't have a monopoly on corruption. In our society, this vice is pretty well diffused. The above should not be interpreted as a rationale for rotten behavior. Rather it should be viewed as a plea to more properly focus blame or praise on the responsible party, instead of resorting to stereotypes and mass condemnations, which are prime tools of the bigot and dictator.

The fact is many corporations are going above and beyond the call of duty in meeting the needs of society. Unfortunately, a vast segment of society is totally unaware of these good works and still another hard-core segment attributes ulterior motives to all corporate behavior.

In many instances, business has done a poor job of merchandising the essentiality of profit. It is not always understood or accepted that profit represents to the firm what the satisfaction of biological needs represents to the individual—i.e., survival. Without food or water, the human being perishes. Without profit, businesses cannot survive. The person locked in a vault with a ten minute supply of oxygen and the vault set to open in four hours is not concerned with love, esteem, or self-actualization. He needs air to live. In a similar fashion, unless a business is able to make a profit, problems of ecology and corporate citizenship, as crucial as they are, can not be properly addressed.

In short, many businesses, after satisfying the basic need for profit, are moving on to other areas. Further, smart entrepreneurs, owners, and managers understand that profit is not an end in itself, just as the rational being does not exist solely to eat or breathe.

The Other Side of Profit is simply an attempt to display the reverse side of the coin. It's not a whitewash. It is a factually accurate description of what certain businesses are doing for people and society.

Quite frankly, we feel that this other side deserves a look and perhaps a bit more exposure than has been customary.

Finally, our sincere thanks and appreciation must be expressed to the following individuals for their support and contribution to this

effort: Jim Ewing, Delta Air Lines; Dennis Mick, Motorola, Inc.;
Robert H. Lane, The Goodyear Tire and Rubber Company; A. D.
Frazier, Jr., The Citizens and Southern National Bank; Patrick J.
Kremer, Eaton Corporation; Carol Bork, James MacGregor, and
Kitter Meade, CBS, Inc.; and Marjorie R. Baroni, Fayette, Mississippi.

LLOYD L. BYARS
MICHAEL H. MESCON

Contents

ROBERT C. GUNNESS

Robert C. Gunness, Vice Chairman of Standard Oil Company (Indiana), joined the staff of the company's Research Department in 1938. He advanced to Assistant Director of Research in 1943, Associate Director in 1945, and Manager of Research in 1947. In 1952 he became Assistant General Manager of Manufacturing. He was elected to the Board of Directors in 1953, and became General Manager of Supply and Transportation in 1954.

Mr. Gunness was named an Executive Vice President in 1956, to direct and coordinate the activities of the manufacturing, sales, and supply and transportation departments. In 1958 he was assigned additional responsibilities, primarily in the field of coordination of activities of some of the company's major subsidiaries. He was elected President in 1965 and was named Vice Chairman February 28, 1974.

Born at Fargo, North Dakota, in 1911, he grew up at Amherst, Massachusetts, where his father was for many years head of the Engineering Department of the University of Massachusetts. After receiving a B.S. degree in chemistry at the University of Massachusetts, he went on to Massachusetts Institute of Technology, where he earned a D.Sc. degree in chemical engineering. He remained at M.I.T. as an Assistant Professor of Chemical Engineering for two years.

In his research work, Mr. Gunness became known as a specialist in distillation and heat transfer. He has been prominent in the development and design of new processes for the refining of petroleum.

In 1951, Mr. Gunness was on leave from Standard Oil Company for several months to serve as Vice Chairman of the research and development board of the Department of Defense in Washington, D.C.

Mr. Gunness is a director of the Harris Trust and Savings Bank, Inland Steel Company, and the American Petroleum Institute. He is a trustee of the University of Chicago, a life member of the Corporation of the Massachusetts Institute of Technology, chairman of the Committee for Corporate Support of American Universities, and a director of the John Crerar Library.

He is also a member of the American Chemical Society and a fellow of the American Institute of Chemical Engineers. From his academic days he has been a member of the Sigma Xi and Phi Kappa Phi honor societies and the Kappa Sigma fraternity. He is a member of the Flossmoor Country Club, the Commercial Club, the Chicago Club, and the Cosmos Club, Washington, D.C.

Chapter **1**

Profitability: The Foundation for Effective Corporate Social Action[1]

ROBERT C. GUNNESS

I would like to consider with you some of the broader aspects of corporate social responsibility, and then try to deal in a pragmatic way with some of the realities of corporate involvement in this sphere. I must confess, at the outset, that I am becoming increasingly uncomfortable with the phrase "corporate social responsibility." It has been much used and abused in recent years, and it is obvious today that it means many different things to different people.

What concerns me most is the fact that to many of our citizens— particularly those most deprived, frustrated, or disillusioned—the phrase implies the belief that corporations have a direct responsibility for the solution of the many problems that plague society and that they have the ability, unilaterally, to solve them.

This, at best, is an unrealistic expectation. At worst, it could actually be counterproductive if it causes society to look to business for actions and solutions of which it is incapable, and that properly are the responsibility of other social and political institutions.

I am sure that most people are familiar with the public opinion polls of recent years which suggest that public desires for business social action are on the rise, but that public confidence that business will respond to these desires has been in a steady decline over much of the past decade.

It is not surprising that people—troubled by conditions in the world in which they live and disillusioned by the failure of government to put them right—should turn to business for solutions. It is,

[1]Much of the material presented here is from a speech given before the National Council on Philanthropy in Detroit, Michigan, on October 23, 1973.

3

after all, the business and industrial sector of our society that has been largely responsible for the standard of living and the overall affluence that our nation enjoys. Also, I suspect, it is the success of business in satisfying the material wants of the vast majority of Americans that has provided them with the luxury of turning their attention to new and higher aspirations. These aspirations involve the quality of life, rather than the quantity of goods, and more humanistic personal goals rather than the traditional ethic of successful and materially rewarding work.

We have, thus, a condition in which the public believes that the skills, techniques, and resources employed by business and industry in the successful achievement of material goals can and should now be turned to the satisfaction of this new order of expectations.

This attitude, it must be confessed, has been encouraged by the rhetoric of some well-meaning business leaders who have accepted a social role for themselves and their corporations far beyond what they reasonably can expect to deliver.

An unrealistic view of corporate social capabilities may also have been fostered by pollsters who have generated expectations simply by suggesting them. I recently read the report of a Louis Harris poll which presented a cross-section of American households with a list of social concerns and asked which of them were matters to which businessmen and companies should give some special leadership. This is a continuing survey that was first made in 1966.

Even recognizing the power of suggestion that was implicit in Mr. Harris' list, I was astonished by the responsibilities that the public apparently expected business executives to assume.

I won't list all of the 16 areas covered by the survey, but I think you will appreciate my dismay when I tell you that 88 per cent of those polled wanted me, and other business executives, to eliminate depressions, 85 per cent wanted me to rebuild the cities, 83 per cent wanted me to wipe out poverty, 76 per cent wanted me to find cures for diseases, 73 per cent wanted me to control crime, and 57 per cent wanted me to cut government red tape.

Even if I were egotistical enough to tackle the first items on that list, I'd have to throw in the towel on the last one.

The lesson to be learned from this poll, it seems to me, is not that business leaders should learn how to perform miracles. Instead, I believe we must begin to use forums to develop, through consensus, an acceptable definition of what the social responsibilities of business really are.

Perhaps we could make some progress toward that objective if we were to look at the business role as one of accountability rather than responsibility. We might start by asking ourselves what business should and must do, and what the public has the right to expect it to do, in order to carry out its still vital economic mission in a socially responsible way.

As an example of what I mean, let me suggest that it is not the unilateral responsibility of American business to clean up the environment, or to determine the standards of environmental quality that the public wants, needs, and is willing to pay for. I say this at some risk because, according to Mr. Harris, 92 per cent of the American people believe that business should assume leadership in cleaning up the environment, even though only 36 per cent believe that it will.

Nevertheless, the fact is that business simply can't assume this responsibility—and shouldn't—because there are too many trade-offs involved. The public, which includes business, must determine through its representatives in government how these trade-offs should be resolved.

This is not to suggest that business has no responsibility for clean air and clean water. The corporation certainly is accountable to the public for the extent to which its own operations are conducted within the environmental standards set by government in behalf of the public. And, I believe, its responsibilities go even farther than that. The corporation should not deliberately construct new facilities that will damage the environment; rather, it should seek to construct facilities which avoid damages. The corporation also has an obligation to see that environmental concerns are given appropriate weight with economic considerations in determining the conduct of corporate affairs. And, finally, it has the responsibility to determine whether the company has any special talents that it could bring to bear in the solution of environmental problems.

I guess what troubles me most is that acceptance by business leadership of "social responsibility" without a clear definition of that responsibility, and without recognizing the limitations on business social action, renders such acceptance as really deceptive. It raises false hopes, and inevitably will lead to greater public disenchantment with our economic system, which neither business nor the nation can afford.

I am also concerned that the apparent reluctance of many businessmen to deal openly and candidly with the limitations on corporate social action may stem, in part, from a growing preoccupation with the "image" of business and the fear that any attempt to define corporate social responsibility may be interpreted as a refusal to assume it.

Every time another pollster reports a decline in public respect for business, a tumult arises inside the business community about the need for corporations to improve their images through educational campaigns, advertising, and the like. This, in turn, spawns a torrent of rhetoric about corporate social responsibility and a flood of advertisements about corporate good works. It also leads to countless conferences among businessmen and between businessmen and other social groups intended to demonstrate that profit is not the only corporate concern.

There is nothing immoral about these speeches, ads, and conferences, per se. Business should toot its own horn when it does something that is worth a toot. The danger is that efforts to create a new "image" may become a substitute within the company for the thing that really counts, which is responsible social behavior in every aspect of corporate operations.

The very word "image" has an unfortunate connotation. It deals with how you want to be perceived, rather than what you really are. American business must concentrate more on behavior—more on what it should try to be rather than how it wants to appear—if it is to achieve a reputation for social performance comparable to the esteem that it has long held for its ability to satisfy material needs.

I have dwelt on this subject because I believe it is crucial to an understanding of the emerging social response that I perceive in our company and in most other large corporations. It is also imperative that we understand what business can't do if we are to make real progress in doing the things that we can. And it is particularly important that we focus on some of the obstacles that must be overcome if real social progress is to be made.

Daniel Yankelovich, another pollster, whose findings have been as illuminating as any, has expressed regret that the corporate social concern of the past seven or eight years grew out of the urban-racial discontent of the mid-1960's. He notes that out of their early experience with the urban crises, most businessmen formed a series of judgments.

> First they came to regard the demands of the public sector as a moral issue of what business ought to do to be a good citizen, rather than as a practical issue of what business had to do to survive and prosper in our society.
>
> Second, business executives, with some notable exceptions, came to regard activities with a social responsibility label as marginal to the day-to-day operations of the business.
>
> Third, they came to regard the question of what and how much to do as largely optional.

Mr. Yankelovich points out—I believe quite correctly—that all three of these conclusions were wrong. The need for corporate social concern is practical as well as moral; it has everything to do with the day-to-day operations of the business; and it is no longer optional for any management concerned with the survival of the corporation.

Nevertheless, as a consequence of these judgments, much of the corporate action that we have identified as socially responsible was simply an extension or redirection of traditional corporate programs. In our philanthropic and community relations programs we began to acknowledge to a larger extent that the entire constituency wasn't white. New organizations, representing the needs of underprivileged minority groups, began to appear on the list of those who benefited from corporate charity, and the public relations department found a man — often black — who could relate to minority groups.

The business response, in short, had little to do with corporate behavior — with the way we ran the company. Rather, the primary thrust was to seek new ways to spend money — but not too much — to support the problem-solving efforts of others, rather than to find ways to make the corporation itself profitably responsible and responsive to emerging social expectations.

I believe, if the business community were to be totally candid about those early efforts, it would have to confess that it acted spontaneously rather than thoughtfully in the hope that the exercise of largesse, along with liberal doses of reassuring rhetoric, would dampen the fires of discontent by providing credible hope that things were about to get better.

That may sound unduly harsh, but it is not meant to be, considering the dramatic and frightening excesses to which management felt an immediate need to respond. When your house is on fire, you don't stop to inspect for faulty wiring; you grab a bucket.

I think it is to the credit of corporate management that we have emerged from that holocaust, and the expedient actions of the moment, into a period of reflection — hopefully to be followed by action more worthy of the talents and resources of American business. We have begun to confront the substantive changes that are necessary within the company itself.

Management, in many companies, has begun to recognize and respond to several elements of social concern that can and will lead to more responsible and responsive corporate social policy:

First, it is now aware, because of the ineffectiveness of many early efforts, that a significant and effective corporate social contribution can be developed only within the framework of the profit system — not as a peripheral and purely philanthropic or moral exercise. This is true because the corporate organization is geared to respond to the demands of the market system and its resources cannot be employed effectively outside that context.

Second, management has reminded itself that its primary mission, as a major element of our political, social, and economic system, is one of providing goods and services that the public wants and needs at prices that it can afford to pay. It cannot assume the responsibilities of other elements of society at the expense of superior performance of its own primary mission.

Third, management has also recognized that its continuing

ability to carry out its primary economic function requires that it take some actions—at the expense of immediate profit—that can only be justified in terms of corporate survival, or in the expectation of profits some years down the road.

Fourth, corporate executives have become alert to the reality that if the company is to maximize its social contribution, the entire organization, not merely a handful of urban affairs experts or social specialists, must be involved. This means that the enunciation of social policies is not enough. They must be reinforced, as corporate economic objectives are, by goal-setting, accountability, performance measurement, and the distribution of penalties and rewards.

I was impressed by some comments on this subject made by James F. Bodine, President of the First Pennsylvania Corporation, at his firm's annual meeting. He said:

> From my observations, most companies have given [social responsibility] a lot of lip service but not much has happened. One reason why not much has happened is, I believe, improper organizational structure. . . . I believe in order to get the job done properly, true responsibility must be immersed in the organization structure. Just as with profit planning, all units must be disciplined to set acceptable social plans. Similarly, as with profit reporting, all units must be required to submit regular reports on implementation of such plans; and, all managers must understand that they will be reviewed and rated on the basis of their social performance, just as they are on their profit performance. . . .

Fifth, it is becoming painfully clear to thoughtful executives that their own historical values, and those of the corporation, must be reexamined in the light of overall value changes within the society and the altered expectations that are apparent in the external environment. The changes we see around us are not mere fads. They are profound, if not cataclysmic, and the institutions of our society that survive will be those with the wisdom, ingenuity, and flexibility to change with the times.

There is little doubt in my mind that in the years ahead, the quality of corporate management will increasingly be judged in terms of the ability of executives to anticipate, respond to, and manage change. The former U.S. Secretary of Commerce, Peter G. Peterson, who is now Chairman of Lehman Brothers, referred to this in a speech in Cincinnati. He said:

> One yardstick I have found useful in assessing the real strength of a company . . . is how much time its very best people could devote to the future. Wherever I saw most or all of the company preoccupied with today's and next month's and even this year's problems—very frequently, I found, it was an enterprise that either was in, or was headed for, trouble.
> Conversely, the best managed corporations, I found, invested substantial amounts of their most precious resource—the time of their top managers—in the future; protecting the future; and defining the problems and the opportunities of the future; and deciding how to best shape the future instead of being shocked by it.

The social responsibility of the corporation, in my judgment, will be closely related to the effort management expends to learn how to manage social change with the degree of skill they have employed in the past to manage scientific and technological change.

Finally, a major effort is emerging within the corporate community to develop strategies of social action, techniques for measuring social costs and benefits, and organizational arrangements capable of responding to social change. This is no easy task because most of the changes that are occurring—technological, economic, political, psychological, and sociological—are inextricably related to each other. They constitute a system that must be dealt with as a system, but most companies have been accustomed to dealing with them individually, in a vertical rather than lateral way. We are still at the bottom of the learning curve as far as our understanding of social systems and of processes for social audits is concerned.

Philanthropy, of course, will have a continuing role in corporate social programs—and I think there is a clear need for corporate donors to become more aware of and involved in the determination of how their dollars are being invested. Simply writing a check to support an institution, a cause, or a project—however worthy it may happen to be—is no longer enough. I think it may be time for us to become as concerned with the management of philanthropic investment as we are with the other investments that we make, and to exercise a prudent degree of oversight over the uses to which such funds are put.

A recent study of corporate social responsibility by the Committee on Economic Development strongly suggests that most of the public believes that corporations are giving enough. What is expected today is not that corporations give more, but that they behave differently. Financial support for minority causes, for example, is not an acceptable substitute for affirmative action in corporate employment and purchasing programs.

Let me turn now, in conclusion, to some of the obstacles and concerns that corporations are encountering in their efforts to define a rational, appropriate, and adequate social role.

A bolt of lightning may strike me dead the next time I walk down Wall Street, but I must put at the top of the list of obstacles to change the pressure exerted by the financial community for a steady increase in earnings-per-share on a quarterly basis. This, in two major ways, has an impact on management's ability to adapt to change, and anticipate future needs.

First of all, the pressure for increased earnings leads to preoccupation with immediate profit maximization, which makes it extremely difficult to justify expenditures that are intended to enhance profits in the long run, rather than in the near term. Enlightened self-interest has become an acceptable rationalization for expenditures that are calculated to insure a profitable future. Unfortunately, however, while the cost of socially responsible acts can almost always be determined, it is rarely possible to quantify their monetary benefits. Whether social costs are in the form of reduced short-term earnings or increased prices of products, how does the company audit social performance to assure shareholders and customers that they are getting their money's worth?

Until a solution to this problem is found there will be severe constraints on corporate social investments—even those that management may deem necessary for corporate survival.

Pressure for short-term earnings also has an impact on corporate social behavior because of the extent to which it dominates the day-to-day management of the company. In most companies, over a long period of time, the entire organization has been geared to respond to short-term profit objectives. Even when top management determines that it is proper to sacrifice short-term profit to achieve long-term goals, it is often difficult to get the organization to respond to the long-term objective.

This is true simply because budgets are drawn, sales objectives are defined, and managerial performance is measured on the basis of immediate profit considerations. Management may express the willingness to sacrifice some short-term profit on a corporate basis, to achieve a social objective. But pity the poor manager who sacrifices profit in his own piece of the corporate operations and seeks to justify it on the basis of corporate social goals. Some rational way must be found to reconcile this conflict.

Some other obstacles to change—and let me tick them off quickly—include:

The preoccupation of most corporate organizations with immediate problems—the kind of crisis management that fails to recognize that today's problems were yesterday's opportunities, if they had been dealt with in time.

Tradition, habit, and a myopic fixation on past successes and failures—"We'll do it that way again, because it worked last time," or "We'll never try that again, because it didn't work before"—both comments made without recognition that the environment in which a previous effort worked or failed isn't with us any more.

Stubborn adherence to traditional values that are no longer the values of society at large.

Let me say simply that these are obstacles that inhibit the ability of the corporation to respond to social needs, and there are many others. But they are only obstacles; they are not insuperable barriers. They are, in short, problems to be solved, and I am confident that we will solve them, because that is what business desires.

My purpose in this chapter has been to develop a better understanding of the realities of corporate social involvement as the basis for a more rational and thoughtful approach to the corporate social role. I recognize that a hazard of my remarks is the possibility that they may be interpreted as an indication that I want to disengage the business community from responsibility in the social sphere.

Let me assure you that this is not the case. On the contrary, I am persuaded that our economic system cannot survive unless those who participate in it engage themselves more fully with society's problems. My concern is that business use its talents to effect real change and improvement in society, rather than apply cosmetics.

What are some of the things business can and must do if it is to make a significant contribution to improving the society in which we live? Let me cite a few actions that I consider basic without, however, suggesting that these are the only options.

First, as I have suggested earlier, every business organization must reexamine its most cherished values to insure that the concepts it considers important are in tune with the values held by society at large. This, in the decades ahead, will be a continuous, evolutionary process, for we are living in an age of social discontinuity in which nothing holds still for very long.

Second, business must reevaluate and modify its long-range planning and decision making processes to insure that it understands the potential social consequences of its acts. We cannot afford unwittingly to lay the booby traps for the future. Something as routine as the decision on where to locate a plant can no longer be treated as a simple economic matter. Management still needs to know the economic consequences, but it also must give full consideration to other factors—ecological consequences and impact on employment opportunities for the disadvantaged are examples.

Third, in cooperation with government and voluntary agencies, business must seek ways in which its technological knowledge, organizational skills and sophisticated systems methodology can be applied to public problems.

Fourth, again in cooperation with government, business must exercise leadership in the development of new forms of organization that can plan for the future and utilize the resources of the private sector to help government achieve long-term goals. Structures in which the concern is with technology, rather than social problems, such as NASA and the Atomic Energy Commission, obviously are easier to develop, but the combined ingenuity of government, the academic community, and business should be able to develop similar devices to deal with other forms of public problems.

Fifth, business must increase its support for the problem-solving efforts of voluntary institutions, not so much in dollars as in providing technical and managerial assistance through the voluntary involvement of its most talented people. Particular emphasis should be given to support for innovative new approaches that address the causes of social problems (not merely deal with the symptoms), that are reproducible, and that will challenge the status quo in education, job training, health care, and other areas where our present approach is out of touch with the times.

Sixth, business must give particular attention to the ways in which, in its own operations, it can help to eliminate the economic disparities that exist in our society. Many of our most frustrating social problems stem from the fact that a substantial segment of the population is economically deprived, not because of individual inadequacy, but because of race, color, or creed.

Business has a unique capacity to deal with these problems. We need to practice affirmative action to insure equal employment opportunity in our own organizations and give leadership to encourage its practice in others. In Chicago, for example, more than a dozen major companies are now sharing minority employment data and have organized and funded a minority employment program that is designed initially to put their own houses in order and ultimately encourage other companies in the city to do likewise.

Similarly, many Chicago firms have turned their attention to ways in which they can influence the employment of minorities by those with whom they do business. We are currently completing a new 80-story headquarters building for our company which is the fourth tallest structure in the world. In the past, minority participation in the construction of a structure of this size has been exceedingly limited. We decided when we undertook this venture that we would make it a model of affirmative action for minority employment in the construction trades, and negotiated the construction contracts with that objective in mind.

As a consequence, throughout construction, more than 30 per cent of the construction workers on the job were members of minority groups. The prime component in achieving this result was a management decision that it needed to be done.

Similar opportunities exist in the development of minority enterprises. For more than 10 years, our company had a corporate policy that we would utilize minority suppliers of goods and services. It took us from 1961 to 1970 to reach a level of about $600,000 a year in purchases from minority suppliers. In 1970 we decided that if we were to make real progress in this area, we would have to do it with the same technique employed to achieve other corporate objectives: the setting of specific annual goals, performance review, and the fixing of individual responsibility on our purchasing agents and line managers.

In the first year, as a result of these actions, we more than tripled our minority purchases, and in the three years since this program began operation we have increased the level of minority purchases more than tenfold.

Many minority firms can be helped simply by providing them with an opportunity to show what they can do. In the construction of our new building we had several examples of this. One relatively small carpet contractor was given the opportunity to install the carpeting for a portion of our building. His demonstration of capable performance has now enabled him to secure the contract for carpeting the entire Sears Tower—the tallest building in the world.

Another example is that of a minority maintenance contractor to whom, about five years ago, we awarded the contract for just one of the buildings at our Naperville Research Center. Subsequently he was awarded a second building at that facility and then a third. Next, we assisted him in gaining union sanction to operate in Chicago's Loop and he began working in a building we own on Michigan Avenue.

If you were to visit our new headquarters building today you would find employees of this minority firm at work throughout the structure. Dale Maintenance, a minority firm, has the maintenance contract for the entire building, which, when the structure is fully completed, will probably have a value in excess of $1 million a year.

In this brief recital of social opportunities available to business, I have by no means exhausted the possibilities. I have not, for example, touched on corporate responsibility in the area of consumerism —a subject so broad that it is not possible for me to deal with it here. I might simply note that, apart from attempting to satisfy legitimate consumer demands, business is going to have to begin to search its conscience to determine the extent to which its decisions may be squandering resources that may better be reserved for future use. Regardless of consumer preferences, some brakes may have to be applied to the rate at which we are using up our dwindling supplies of minerals and other natural resources.

Let me close by saying that, despite some of the reservations that I have expressed about the social capabilities of business, and despite the disenchantment that is apparent in some quarters, I have great confidence in the future of American business, and in its ability to contribute to continued progress—both economic and social—in America and in the world. But I also share with Ray Bauer of Harvard University, who has been a leader in the development of corporate social indicators, the view that we are in the midst of an evolution in defining what we mean by progress. The new definition will be couched more in human and environmental terms, less directly in terms of economics, technology, and gross production of goods and services.

As a businessman, I don't find that frightening. It gives me hope.

WILLIAM THOMAS BEEBE

W. T. (Tom) Beebe is Chairman of the Board and Chief Executive Officer of Delta Air lines.

A native of Los Angeles, California, Mr. Beebe has been in the airline industry since he joined Chicago and Southern Air Lines on February 20, 1947, in charge of all personnel and labor relations. He was made a Vice President of C & S on January 1, 1951. After the merger of Delta and C & S on May 1, 1953, he served as Personnel Director of the combined company. He was elected Vice President on April 13, 1954, and to the Board of Directors on September 14, 1966. He was elevated to Senior Vice President–Administration on November 1, 1967, was elected President on January 22, 1970, and became Chairman of the Board and Chief Executive Officer on November 1, 1971.

Mr. Beebe is a graduate of the University of Minnesota, where he majored in business administration. For 10 years prior to joining C & S he had extensive personnel and labor relations experience with General Electric and with United Aircraft Corporation. During the war he was in charge of personnel administrative and labor relations activities at the U.S. Navy owned Pratt & Whitney Aircraft company of Missouri at Kansas City.

He is a member of the All Saints Episcopal Church, and on the Boards of Directors of the Air Transport Association, Citizens & Southern National Bank, Citizens & Southern Realty Investors, Provident Life & Accident Insurance Company, and LectraData, Inc. He is on the National Advisory Council of the Multiple Sclerosis Society and is a former member of the Atlanta Board of Education.

Chapter 2

Delta—A Ready Heart

TOM BEEBE

In the American marketplace, probably no competition is stronger than that which exists between the stockholder-owned and operated airlines. The only product the airlines have to sell is themselves and their reputation for dependable, personalized service and safety.

This is true because of a number of factors, including the airlines' unique status as public carriers subject to government control over their ability to set rates and fares, their operational procedures and their route structures. They are dependent upon two federal agencies, the Civil Aeronautics Board and the Federal Aviation Administration, for their ability to conduct business. At the same time, they often fly the same type of airplanes over similar routes, charge the same fares, and share a multitude of similar procedures, even "language." They are tied together by computers vis-à-vis ticketing, reservations, and flight information. They manufacture no new and varied products which can be displayed to the public at annual events or in everyday showrooms.

Even so, since World War II the airlines have established a transportation system in the United States which is the world's envy. Domestic nonstop and through plane schedules, supplemented by interline connections, now allow businessmen, vacationers, and shippers to travel between cities and nations on the world's finest equipment in a manner and at speeds which were believed impossible just a quarter of a century ago. They have literally changed the style of American life, helped create new industries, and provided thousands of jobs for their own companies and for their related service industries. Their impact on the American economy in salaries, purchases and construction is a hallmark of the nation's free enterprise system.

This bright picture is clouded by inflationary pressure, increased operational costs, staggering outlays for new equipment—airplanes (the "third generation wide-body" jets which deliver at costs exceeding $15 million each), computers, flight simulators, facilities, airport areas—and by vastly increased environmental protection regulations and fuel costs. Even though faced with these problems, the airlines must produce a return for stockholders, pay salaries, and set aside funds for future expansion and purchases. The miracle is that they have accomplished so much in a relatively few years and have still remained viable.

The years between 1970 and 1974 have been difficult ones at best for the United States airlines. Only a few of the trunk carriers have consistently managed profitable operations. Most have suffered sizeable losses, and nearly all have amassed huge debt responsibilities. For several, the financial future is a grim era to contemplate.

But the airline business can be profitable. Delta Air Lines is a good example.

Delta Air Lines, based in Atlanta, Georgia, the hub of a vast and rapidly expanding "Southeast Economic Empire," has shown a profit almost every year since the start of its passenger service in 1929. It has operated profitably for the past 26 consecutive years, even during the economic strictures of the period. In the recessionary period of 1970–1971, Delta reported steady and growing profits while some other airlines were forced to curtail operations, were strike-bound, or had to furlough or release employees. In the fiscal year ended in June, 1971, Delta reported earnings in excess of $30 million, more than the combined earnings of all the domestic trunk airlines. Since then, it has broken its own records and, in the fiscal year ended in June, 1973, reported all-time new high earnings of more than $60 million. In operating revenues, it reached the billion dollar standard during the same period. The airline is widely recognized for broad-based management ability, an excellent safety record, good service, and an unusually close knit, company-minded employee "family."

While Delta was busily accomplishing its financial goals and paying steady dividends, it was also in the process of ordering and accepting delivery of an entire new fleet of airplanes, 42 Boeing 727's (with the wide-body interior configuration), five Boeing 747's, 30 advanced technology Lockheed L–1011 "TriStars," and five DC–10's. It was buying or installing a new generation of computers and computer allied machinery for its "Deltamatic" reservations system, and it was building or redesigning new passenger and maintenance facilities in many of its cities. In Atlanta, it completed the third major expansion of its jet overhaul base, a sprawling one mile long facility. At considerable expense, it has equipped its DC–9 and original Boeing 727 fleets, totalling over 100 airplanes, with environmental control equipment. Most important, it has a steady record of paying above-average salaries to its personnel.

Delta's financial strength was forcefully demonstrated when, in 1970, it appeared that the Lockheed TriStar program might be abruptly terminated because of problems incurred by its engine manufacturer, the Rolls-Royce Company of England. Rolls-Royce announced suddenly that it would be unable to deliver the TriStar's RB.211 engines at the contract price, if at all. As an interim protective move, Delta promptly ordered five McDonnell Douglas DC–10's at a total order price exceeding $70 million. It was prepared to buy even more. Few airlines could display such a degree of planning flexibility under such difficult circumstances. Instead of furloughing personnel during that uneasy period, Delta enlarged its payroll to meet a future its management knew was almost at hand.

Then, on August 1, 1972, Delta announced a merger with financially ailing Northeast Airlines and prepared to join the strenuous "Northeast corridor to Florida/Bahamas competition." Eastern and National, respecting Delta's proven "track record," fought hard and long to remain "Delta free." The merger, when approved by the CAB, added 3,500 new employees, service to over 20 new cities, and thousands of new route miles to the Delta system. It gave Delta an unparalleled opportunity to tie New England to the South and Southeast and opened new markets which the airline had sought for many years. Lest there be a mistaken opinion, however, Delta was not "awarded" the merger as a prize for a job well done. It negotiated the Northeast merger at a price which few other airlines or corporations were then in a position to match.

Delta is known in the industry as a "vigorous competitor" which makes few mistakes. When, some years ago, many trunk airlines told the Civil Aeronautics Board that their service to small cities caused a financial drain and asked that their service be terminated at a host of such cities, Delta increased its service to its multitude of small to medium hubs with an entire new fleet of DC–9's. It operates the shortest stagelength routes of any trunk airline in the nation.

The result? Delta's plethora of small to medium hub cities "feed" passengers to its long-haul routes and pay off handsomely. New York's financial community regards the airline as "thoroughly professional" and gives it high marks for its expertise, passenger service and management ability. It is consistently regarded as a good investment. Delta's retention of passengers, those who "return to fly again," a critical industry factor, is considered a world standard.

"Advertising did it all for Delta?" Not so. Delta is known as a "low key" advertiser, not given to "blue sky" lineage. A Madison Avenue advertising executive described Delta's advertising program, centered mainly in the published media, as "grocery ads, but ads which tell a passenger what he needs to know. That is simply where the flights go, what time they leave, and how much they cost to get there." Delta also exhibits a fetish for immaculate and expertly maintained modern airplanes. Moreover, Delta exerts every effort to be completely honest with its customers. "If a flight seems destined to be delayed," a Delta ticket supervisor said recently, "we don't scrub the flight and set up a new number as some do. We just delay it, and we try to tell the passengers exactly why it was delayed and what to expect." And it does appear that this direct approach has not hurt the company's passenger retention.

Some analysts feel Delta's profitability might have hurt it at times in a vital area, i.e., route decisions of the Civil Aeronautics Board, for the airline has received few major route awards since 1960 (when it was certified to operate across the "Southern Tier," beyond Dallas to Nevada and California). Indeed, many of the CAB's recent decisions have placed competition on major Delta routes.

But, to date, this competition has not seriously affected Delta's growth. For example, in Atlanta, Delta's major competitor, Eastern, operates more daily flights than does Delta, an airline noted for "cautious scheduling." But Delta still outboards Eastern every month in Atlanta by considerable margins, although both airlines operate basically the same type of airplanes and share similar facilities.

How, then, does Delta, facing new competition, increased operating costs, new aircraft deliveries and orders, inflationary pressures, and other economic woes which have buffeted the industry, not only survive but prosper?

If we have a "business secret," it is the caliber of our people. Admittedly, we also have a fine area in which to operate, a good climate for business in the Southeast, a strong management group whose working lives together total several centuries of Delta longevity, a hard-working and interested Board of Directors, and supportive and friendly bankers. But our finest possessions are our own people, Delta's family of employees, and the most loyal passengers and friends in the history of the airline business. Our people are a close-knit family, albeit a big one. But the loyalty is there, the same as in any family. It is a family with a heart. Delta people frequently say that they don't have a job, they have a way of life. This sincerity and enthusiasm is extended to passengers who quickly realize that here are 28,000 people who will "go the extra mile" for them at every opportunity, whose ambition in life must be service to other people.

Are Delta's people really different? I believe that they are. For example, a flight crew may see that an airplane might incur a delay because of a luggage or cleaning problem. What happens? Pilots help with the luggage and flight attendants help clean the airplane. Most passengers never know the extent of those "behind the scenes" activities.

"We have a motto here," a stewardess told a writer not long

ago. "It's 'maximum utilization of all personnel and equipment.' We work. It works. We couldn't do without it. It's the difference between us and somebody else."

Heart? Never a week passes that letters from appreciative passengers aren't received in our offices in praise of our personnel "because, well, you won't believe this, but do you know that one of your stewardesses actually took my kid sister to her house and let her stay there until the snow storm let up and the airplanes could fly again?..."

Heart? During the 1970–1971 recessionary period, a number of Delta's Atlanta personnel became concerned that the financial unrest could have a detrimental effect on the number of passengers boarded. They also had heard the boast of a major competitor to the effect that "We are going to outboard Delta here in its own home town." On their own initiative, Delta's people—ticket agents, ramp agents, mechanics, passenger service agents, stewardesses, pilots and many others—then formed a committee for action. They set up a working staff among themselves, volunteered to make calls on and contacts with Atlanta businesses, then asked for management's blessings and guidance. It was a fascinating accomplishment. Management suddenly found that it has over a thousand volunteer marketing representatives ready to plow the field. The committee, now called "CDRC" (Customer Development and Retention Committee), was so successful that we have retained it as an active volunteer arm of Delta's marketing effort. This is an off-duty enterprise. Pilots are actively engaged in making marketing calls in a special annual program. Flight attendants volunteer as "career day" speakers in hundreds of high schools and colleges in hopes of recruiting future Delta candidates.

... And more heart! Several years ago, Delta's people in a number of cities took notice that military "standby" passengers, service personnel traveling on reduced rate, space available tickets, and those on leave or liberty or those in transit between duty stations, were often stranded during rush hour periods and during the holiday times. There was little for the service personnel to do in lonely airports. "If only we could think of some way to help," our employees said.

They found a way. In Atlanta, they approached the company's station manager, secured a little-used room in Delta's concourse area, and established the nation's first airport "Military Lounge." Delta personnel from every department brought stereo equipment, a television set, and furniture. They decorated the room and provided it with coffee pots, cakes, pies, cookies, and soft drinks. On their own time and in off-duty hours, they staffed the room and helped make the Atlanta stopovers pleasant memories for thousands of the nation's service personnel. Military lounges have now been "taken over" by the airline as permanent Delta facilities, but they are still staffed by Delta volunteers.

This is the heart of a great corporation. Surely it is a key to Delta's success, and it is a more important key than all the new airplanes, computers, and facilities that money could buy.

Does an airline or a corporation decide to create esprit de corps and heart? Does it send a directive letter to its people stating, "Here's a new angle. If we are nice to people, perhaps they'll be nice to us. Perhaps they'll buy our products or flock to our ticket counters and airplanes. Let's start right now."

Or is "heart" an unseen force evolved over many years?

A Delta reservations agent described her feelings toward the company. "We know Delta is behind us. We are a part of it. Our voices count. We know also from experience that a world of opportunity exists here. There's room for advancement on every hand. If we work hard and honestly, we'll get promotions and salary increases just as surely as the sun rises. What's more, management won't bring outsiders in to fill supervisory openings. Our company lives its promotion-from-within policy and makes it work every day." The agent added, "We don't need two people when one of us can get the job done. We are very proud of that. You might call it a trust that exists between us and management. But when you look at it another way, we are a part of management. As far as we are concerned, we love Delta and are only doing our job."

This philosophy is quickly transmitted to new personnel by the "older hands," for those people work as friends and confidants. "If we encounter trouble in our personal lives, there's good old Delta to step in and help out," the same agent said. "I think the company would rather perish than see one of its people hurt. If we've got a gripe, the supervisor will listen. Mr. Beebe's door is always open. There are no secrets here at Delta. We'll pull together no matter what. If that's old-fashioned, thank God for it."

How does a job come to be a way of life?

Delta's heritage is a rich one. It started long ago in north Louisiana. Delta's people, across the years, picked up the story and took it to their hearts. Some have said, "the heritage is beautiful." Whatever it is, it has brought Delta a greatness undreamed of in ordinary hours. It is literally a part of their past, and their hopes and dreams of the future, one of unchallenged and bountiful opportunity.

To understand the Delta spirit and its heart, one has to travel back across the years to Monroe, Louisiana, and the early 1930's when the company operated Huff-Daland cotton dusters and several small passenger airplanes. A Delta employee from Monroe, who was

"12 years old before he knew anything else other than a Delta airplane flew," tells his company's story.

You might say that Delta is a product of the people and the area from which it came. It is impossible to tell of its life story without recalling something of its birth and childhood. Whether they realize it or not, every member of Delta's employee family old or new now bears something of the stamp, "Made in Monroe, Louisiana."

Monroe lies in the center of north Louisiana, not far south of Arkansas, some eighty miles west of Vicksburg and a hundred miles east of Shreveport. From Monroe to Vicksburg and on northward to the delta country of Mississippi, the land is low and flat, filled from one end to the other with cotton fields. The fields are broken now and then by cypress-lined bayous or patches of moist forest. If you know of the geography of the area or had talked to the oil and gas people, you could perhaps imagine the wide bay which once extended from the Mississippi River cliffs near Vicksburg to the high banks on the west side of the Ouachita.

If you've been there, you'll know that the Ouachita is one of the world's most beautiful rivers. It meanders through Arkansas, crosses the Louisiana line north of Bastrop, comes by Monroe, and then joins the Black and the Red Rivers to flow into the Mississippi above Baton Rouge.

In summer, it is hot in that country. But it's a lazy, not unpleasant hot. Life still moves along pleasantly in Monroe even as it did in the old times. Though Monroe and West Monroe, the "Twin Cities," are now bigger, and the tempo is a bit faster, you could almost see, if you looked hard enough, the area as it was in 1930, the early days of Delta.

You probably couldn't starve in that country. People are so friendly and concerned. They wouldn't let you. What's more, the area is a world of wildlife and fish. In winter, ducks and wildfowl regard Black Bayou and "Wham Break" as a vacationland. Many of them must come there to retire. Bass, speckled perch (sometimes called "crappie"), and many other varieties of fish live in the bayous, rivers, and lakes. In the old days, you could sit on the wooden bridge across Phillips Bayou. Hundreds of cypress trees grew out of the water, and fish would come up to break the mirror surface. It was a good time. Even if depression-poor, people somehow managed to live a fine, full life. They pulled together because they had to. On Sundays, people would boat up the Ouachita to Long John Silver, a wide, sandy river beach. Youngsters scampered on the sand and Dad would read Fred Williamson's beautifully written editorials and stories in the *Sunday World*. Captain Cooley's old river boat rested quietly in the water nearby, and at night there were bonfires and bright stars. There was an ancient Indian mound on the Cole Plantation. From the top of the mound, it seemed as high as heaven and we could look across the cotton fields of home.

Into those fields in the early days came the boll weevil. Here was a stealthy invader from Mexico, a long, spear-snouted insect which sat back and waited until the little cotton plant produced a boll. The weevils would then bore and eat in, lay eggs, and destroy the boll. In the space of only a few years, boll weevils nearly destroyed the southern cotton industry.

But the boll weevils reckoned without the airplane and some visionary pioneers—C. E. Woolman, an agricultural extension agent; Dr. Bert Coad, an agronomist; C. E. Faulk, a publisher; Travis Oliver, a Monroe banker; and Print Atkins, a hardware store owner. There were also a group of ex-military pilots and a near-defunct airplane manufacturing company. Woolman and

Coad believed that the airplane could be put into the fight against weevils. There had been some earlier and successful agricultural flying. You might think, however, of Woolman and Coad as the "Billy Mitchells" of agricultural aviation. Because of their determination and ingenuity and the support of the local people, a company was formed. The battle lines against weevils were joined. A heritage was started.

It was a battle in those days, one against little money and plenty of weevils. Woolman also believed that airplanes could make money carrying passengers. That was an outlandish dream when you considered the airplanes then in existence. They carried only a few passengers on short flights. But the company was formed, townspeople and backers had faith, and the early Delta company reached out for life.

Back in those times, the "General Office" and hangar were located at Monroe's Selman Field. The field was a gravel, east-to-west strip. It was east-to-west because of the prevailing winds. Later on, the strip was paved. Delta Air Corporation, as it had been renamed from the original "Huff-Daland Dusters, Inc.," owned only 13 dusters, called "Puffers," an OX–5 "Travelaire," an OX–"Commandair," and a Curtis "Pusher." That was the fleet in 1930! The Puffers were used for dusting while the other airplanes were used in student training and emergency work such as spotting breaks in power lines. They were also engaged in some passenger work between Jackson, Monroe, and Dallas.

"Delta" then was Mr. Woolman, Dr. Coad, Miss Catherine FitzGerald (the secretary whose idea it was to call the company "Delta" after the river delta country nearby), Doug Culver, Chief Pilot Pat Higgins, and pilot Henry Elliot. Delta had one mechanic, a man named Alvin Calhoun. As the operation was seasonal, the company would hire pilots and mechanics as they were needed. Delta's dusters flew "on unit" out of Monroe, Greenwood, Mississippi, and the TVA's Muscle Shoals station in Alabama. Earlier Delta had dusted in Mexico and Peru. In Peru, Woolman helped lay the groundwork for what later was to become the Panagra system.

Monroe in those days was a town of some 20,000 people. There were an iron bridge across the Ouachita and a railroad bridge built by Italian laborers before the turn of the century. Some of their descendants have become many of the city's most prominent citizens. The business section was five blocks long, from "Five Points," near the Illinois Central station, along DeSiard Street, to the river. The main industries were cotton and carbon black. The Brown family built a paper mill across the river. Monroe seemed a quiet little city, but underneath it was a dynamo. People there had foresight and remarkable determination. The city believed in Delta. Now—today—Monroe still believes in Delta. People there think of it as their own, a kind of child of the city. They have a "there goes our boy" attitude, and when you think of it, they are right. At Delta, then, everyone had to pull together and do each other's jobs, because the times were very hard. We helped people just as they helped us.

Then there came a big day in 1934. Delta got the mail contract award, "AM–24." It was front page news in the *Morning World*. With the mail contract in its hands, Delta had to have some larger airplanes. Soon came three Stinson "T's." These were high-wing airplanes, and they carried seven passengers each. With the aircraft, Delta also got some new regular pilots— Charlie Dolson (later to become Delta's Board Chairman and Chief Executive Officer), Don Dice, Lee McBride, George Sheely, Beverly Dickerson, and Bill Miles. O. B. Deere and Miles joined Delta as mechanics. Pilots helped maintain airplanes. Mechanics learned to fly for emergencies. Aboard the Stinsons, pilots served coffee and sandwiches to the passengers. Nearly everyone, including Woolman, sold tickets. Delta's financial backers helped to sell stock and enthusiasm. There was quickly established a policy of "no layoffs" even in the hardest times. Delta people came to appreciate each other in a way which has not stopped. Never was there a finer or more dedicated group of people.

Those were great days, even fantastic days. Delta's routes were extended to Atlanta and on beyond to Charleston. Westward, it started operations into Fort Worth. Then came the low-wing Stinsons, Lockheed's original "Electras," DC–2's and, just before World War II, DC–3's. The corporate headquarters moved to Atlanta, but the dusting division stayed behind in Monroe. During the war, Delta operated only a few DC–3's in passenger service.

Delta, in fact, is a story in three parts. While the original company was grasping for life in Monroe, Carleton Putnam, a New Yorker and Princeton graduate, at his first glimpse of an airplane, immediately perceived a vocation in aviation for himself. He went to California and started an airline. It, too, fought for life, thrived and later moved to Memphis to become the vital Chicago and Southern Air Lines. C & S was not only an airline, it was a generator of energetic, enthusiastic, and amazing people. In 1953, the original Delta and C & S brought about a merger. It was to be one of the most successful airline marriages in the history of the industry because it combined Delta's financial strength and enthusiasm with the unusual C & S élan. It added thousands of new miles, new cities, and new routes to the Midwest, the Caribbean and South America. Bigger and better airplanes came— Lockheed Constellations, DC–7's, and Convair 440's. The merged carrier system was extended into the critically important eastern seaboard (New York, Philadelphia, and Washington/Baltimore).

The new Delta soon pioneered the jet age with the first DC–8's, and Convair 880's. It then pioneered another superior aircraft type, the versatile DC–9. More people joined the company. The "old hands" trained new ones and brought them along in the Delta tradition.

In 1961, routes were extended beyond Dallas to the West and California. It was more than anyone back in Monroe could believe. Delta made its mark on the "Big Board," the New York Stock Exchange.

Meanwhile, up in New England, in the early 1930's, Amelia Earhart and a group of aviation enthusiasts had also formed an airline. It was to become Northeast, based in Boston. Northeast's people had much in common with those of Delta—resilience, quiet determination, and expertise learned in the difficult operational areas of New England. Woolman explored a merger between Delta and Northeast. That was prior to Delta's route extension into New York and Washington. The two route systems lacked a junction point and the first merger attempt with Northeast was halted. But nearly 40 years later, in August, 1972, Delta and Northeast did merge successfully. It was a second good "marriage," one which has opened an unlimited future for the all-new Delta, one with more than 34,000 miles of routes to 99 cities located in 29 states and five foreign nations.

When you think of it, however, not much has really changed. Delta people still pull together just as they did in 1930. There are many new faces and ideas. Airplanes have "grown." But Delta's respect for its employee family and what they can do for others hasn't been altered an inch from the early days, because the C & S and Northeast people brought with them the same philosophy and determination. Delta has only itself in this business. Of course, that's quite a "package." You can spot Delta people across a football field. They haven't forgotten humanity or the fact that in their pursuit of industry success, they are dealing with the hopes and feelings of those with whom they come in contact. It is an amazing organization. We love it. Management would have to run us off!

There is a fair measurement of industrial strength in a realistic assessment of corporate "heart." C. E. Woolman, a major founder and for years Delta's Board Chairman and Chief Executive Officer, died in 1966. Woolman, more than being just a "boss," was considered a well-loved friend by the thousands of company personnel. Shortly after his death, an employee committee was formed to decide on a suitable memorial. The search for such a concept proved to be difficult, for "the Boss" had been a Delta symbol for many years. His concepts of thrift, hard work, and honesty had been the guideposts along Delta's skyroad to success. Then someone remembered that in the dusting division hangar at Monroe were still gathered the remnants of two Huff-Daland "Puffers." Delta owned the patents to the Huff-Dalands and, in fact, frequently built those airplanes in its Monroe shops. "Why not restore a duster and find a suitable place for it? What a memorial that would be." The idea was broached to the Smithsonian Institution in Washington. Response was fast and favorable. "Rebuild the duster," the Smithsonian said, "and there will be a place for it here."

Shortly thereafter, two vans delivered the airplanes to Atlanta. They were little more than a jumble of aircraft skeletons and parts, but the collection was installed in a hangar adjacent to Delta's Atlanta Line Maintenance facility. Under the supervision of Gene Berry, once a duster mechanic, the rebuilding process was started. Nothing was left to chance. Original plans were reviewed and the old mechanical parts were sent across the Atlanta Airport runway to the airline's jet maintenance base, one of the nation's largest, for reconstruction. All wooden parts were exactingly restored to new brightness. The fuselage metal work was restored. Landing gear shock absorbers were patiently reground just as they had been originally formed in the late 1920's. The wings and fuselage were covered in new fabric, doped, and spray painted in the original silver. The familiar red triangle insignias, authentic in every detail, were repainted on the fuselage sides just as they had appeared "on unit" in the battle against boll weevils. It was a project which spanned several months.

The Huff-Daland duster, spanking new again, was rolled out of its hangar in mid-1967 to be photographed adjacent to Delta's new jets. After ceremonies, which were attended by personnel and their friends and relatives from nearly every system city, the duster was shipped to the Smithsonian's Air and Space Museum.

More important than the memorial concept and even the completed project are "how it was done" and "who did it." Delta volunteers, on their own time and in off-duty hours, restored the airplane.

They competed for the opportunity to take even a small part in the project. Like acolytes, they patiently served the restoration. Jet engine mechanics studied the original engine specifications for guidance. Metal workers, more familiar with 500-mile-per-hour jet wing sections, became wood workers. Secretaries and office personnel sewed fabric. The jet upholstery shop built new cockpit fittings according to exact plans. Delta's expert painters sprayed the duster. Those who saw the restoration work in progress reported that it seemed a "joyous experience."

The Woolman Memorial is important to any understanding of Delta's success because it points to an extraordinary cohesiveness among its people. No one was asked to donate time. But during the project there was barely room for the horde of volunteers who even flew in from other cities to work on days off. When the duster was completed, Lead Mechanic Gene Barry said, "It's better than a new one. It could fly right now and start dusting again. That is really no surprise, because we knew Delta's people could do the job." Berry was the only Delta employee assigned full time to the project by management. "Our people," he said, "did this because they respected Mr. Woolman, and they love this company. If you go to the Smithsonian and see the duster, you will see a lot of Delta there. You might also wonder why we couldn't have added a bayou-bordered cotton field complete with a good supply of boll weevils!"

A company is only as strong as its personnel; likewise, a nation's strength is the devotion of its citizens to a national purpose. Some corporations and nations are honored in history. Most never find a page. In future times, if and when a comprehensive history of the airline industry is written, Delta will almost certainly occupy a prominent section. Why? Because its people started the story and are still writing it.

The impact of a corporation on a community is too often measured in dollars and cents. "Local payrolls in Atlanta reached the $100 million mark in the last fiscal year," the news release stated. "Fuel purchases amounted to millions of dollars at the airport," and "thirty cents of each corporate dollar returns to city's coffers," they add. Is economic might of new employees hired, new homes, cars, and refrigerators bought, the only manner in which a corporation can adequately manifest itself?

Surely that economic might is beneficial, but even more so is "People Power," or as some call it, "People Gold"—although the value of people easily transcends that of any precious metal.

For all its economic power, the full measure of corporate impact of any community is people: scoutmasters, church leaders, YMCA volunteers, Little League coaches, volunteer firemen, hospital board members, charity fund raisers tirelessly pounding streets on prospect calls, college endowment chairmen, thousands of people seeking the betterment of their community and their lives in countless ways.

Delta personnel have never needed management urging to join such projects. An army of mayors, church leaders, Scout organizations, Little Leagues, children's homes and beneficial organizations in more than a hundred cities will quickly attest to "the value of having Delta in our midst."

It is sometimes the unseen, untold factors which count the heaviest. An opinion widely held by Delta's competitors maintains that "Delta people will do anything to get passengers and keep them." We submit that the opinion should be restated to read, "Delta people will do anything to help passengers."

Last year, an astonished customer service executive received a letter from a Georgia writer. It said, "I don't know whom to write at Delta, so I'm writing you. Let me tell you what happened. I was driving from my home near Macon to Atlanta to meet my husband. The Macon airport was fogged in. My husband had called to tell me that he would wait for me in Atlanta. Just past Griffin, on the expressway, something happened to the engine in my car. I don't know what it was, but we had to stop. It was very dark and foggy, and we were afraid. We really didn't know what to do. But then, a station wagon pulled up behind my car and a man got out. Turned out that he was a Delta man, because he was wearing a ticket agent's uniform. He checked my car, showed me his Delta identification, and suggested that we ride with him to his home nearby and stay there until he could help get the car repaired. He said he hoped someone would do the same thing for his wife sometime, and then he took us to his house. His wife made us comfortable, and we called my husband. In the meantime, the Delta man saw to it that my car was repaired and had it delivered back to his house. Then he followed us to the airport. He had a bumper sticker on his car which reminded us to 'Fly Delta's Big Jets.' I can promise you that when we fly, we certainly will. Thank you so much for your wonderful man."

Above and beyond the call of duty? Consider tragic times. On July 31, 1973, a Delta DC–9 was approaching Logan International Airport in Boston. In heavy fog, it crashed into a seawall. There was only one survivor, an Air Force sergeant. Delta people across the entire system regarded this as a personal tragedy. They called Atlanta from every system city asking to be allowed to take their leave time to fly to Boston and stay with the families of crash victims. When they heard that the survivor, Sergeant Leopold Chuinard, was terribly burned and needed blood and skin grafts, management in Atlanta was besieged by scores of calls from Delta fellow employees who asked to fly immediately to Boston in hopes of donating blood and even skin.

The father of a young crash victim wrote David C. Garrett, Jr., Delta's president, one of the most moving letters ever written to an airline. "Your people in Boston," the bereaved father said, "could not have been more considerate or helpful. . . . I can't thank your organization enough. They are a fine group and you should be proud of them. . . . You preside over a great airline with probably the best record of all. I thought you might like to hear from one who went through this tragedy as it might help you through this very difficult time in your company's history. I know you are a very closely knit organization, and a tragedy of this type would affect a group like yours more than it would others. . . ."

"Delta's people," a passenger recently wrote, "are fine humans. That, I thinks, sets them apart. They arê not ordinary corporate people. I feel a certain confidence when I am aboard a Delta airplane. It is more than just Delta's professional expertise. It is a knowledge that if I should encounter personal difficulties, I know Delta will respond. That is why I fly Delta. . . ."

When management receives letters directed to individual employees, the letter is placed in that individual's file as a permanent record. The "good letter" files, compiled and published, would fill many volumes. Often as not, the good deeds are cited in Delta's employee magazine, "The Delta Digest."

Other passenger correspondence can help unlock more of the airline's "big secrets."

Andrew E. Ridley, Anniston, Alabama, wrote, ". . . A friend of my family's remarked about Delta's consideration. 'They are beautiful people.' To this I wholeheartedly agree. Before, I had always recommended Delta, but now, more than ever. Delta is Number One in my book. They make one regain faith in humanity and the corporate structure of the public services. However, special, special, and most special thanks should go to Mr. Alvin Whiteside and another Delta agent who stayed at the hospital until my friend was officially pronounced dead of a heart attack. They were two beautiful human beings who didn't think twice about rendering aid and special consideration to us. . . ."

All airlines are basically alike. Fares are the same between cities. The 747's and DC–9's are virtually the same, no matter what colors they wear. Only people make the difference. Kennerd H. Morgenstern, Ph.D., of Westbury, New York, agreed. "My son and his friend were stranded at the airport in Manchester, New Hampshire, late on the evening of December 13, due to a slight misunderstanding on the part of my stepbrother who was to meet them there. Obviously, the mothers of both boys were extremely concerned that their sons were stranded there late at night with no likelihood of being picked up. . . . Unexpectedly and fortunately, Mr. Arthur Lamontagn, one of Delta's personnel at the airport, came to their rescue. He was not only most helpful in discussing with my wife travel plans from Manchester to Bromley, but when it became evident that there was no way to get them there late at night, Mr. Lamontagn was kind enough to bring the boys to his home and put them up for the night. The next day, he and his wife not only provided them with breakfast and lunch, they entertained them until the bus departed late that afternoon. He succeeded in salvaging the boys' ski vacation and saved all the parents involved from much worry. . . ."

Mrs. Francis Patterson, of Charlotte, North Carolina: "My father was traveling on Delta Air Lines and somehow got lost. He is an old man and very nervous. Your Mr. David Cooper got my telephone number from my father and called me at 11:00 P.M. He told me that my father was there and he would try to help him. He told me not to worry about him, that he was going to take my father home to spend the night, and he did. Mr. Cooper took such good care of my father. I just had to write you. . . ."

E. S. Ott, Delta's Station Manager in Detroit, cited one of his ticket counter agents, "A customer approached our ticket counter with a special problem. She was traveling from Frankfurt, Germany, to Miami, Florida, via New York. Because of the weather at Kennedy Airport, the flight had been diverted to Detroit, and she had been re-routed to our Flight 151 to Miami. She and her two-month-old infant had been traveling for over 16 hours and she had exhausted her supply of cereal and formula and was unable to locate any in the terminal. Passenger Service Agent G. DeBolt remembered that one of our employees had just become a father. He called this off-duty employee at his home and advised him of the problem. Senior Customer Service Agent Gerrold Hisey immediately prepared a quantity of formula, secured some cereal, and brought it to the airport. He recognized an individual in need and 'went that extra mile.' . . ."

Mrs. Russell Rosette, of Marysville, Ohio, didn't know whom to thank when she wrote, "On April 18th, my husband and I took our two children, aged nine and sixteen, on their first flight. Our son, nine, is a muscular dystrophy child and was in a wheelchair. When my husband had purchased the tickets earlier, he stated that Robbie would be making his first trip by airplane and that he was in a wheelchair. While we were waiting to board the airplane, the boarding agent, I do not have his name, came over to my husband and asked him if he might present Robbie with a box. In the box was a cake decorated with the words, 'Have a happy flight, Robbie.' Our son was thrilled beyond words and so were we. I do not want this act of kindness to go unnoticed. . . ."

Mr. William DeBruhl, of Asheville, North Carolina, wrote, "I would like to say 'many thanks' to Delta Air Lines and especially to

Mr. Ted Endsley, Passenger Agent, at Love Field, Dallas. My wife and I were flying Delta out of Dallas to Atlanta. While in the boarding area at Love Field, my wife suffered a partial stroke. Mr. Endsley assisted me by calling an ambulance, going to St. Paul's hospital with us, and making reservations for me at a motel nearby. After a few days at the hospital, my wife was released, and Mr. Endsley again assisted us aboard the airplane and had a wheelchair meet us in Atlanta. Never in all my travels have I met a more conscientious person so dedicated to his job and to helping his fellow man. . . .''

Mrs. Lynn W. Turner, Bloomington, Illinois, wrote to thank Passenger Agent Tony DeCourval who had helped in a time of special tragedy, ''Perhaps your personnel are all of Mr. DeCourval's caliber. If so, you are to be congratulated, for he gave service 'above the call of duty.' Needless to say, we shall fly Delta again whenever we can. . . .''

Two Delta agents, John Dean of Boston, and J. W. Williamson of Atlanta, opened their hearts to Mrs. Geraldine Tumminelli of Methuen, Massachusetts. Her husband had suddenly passed away and her son was in Atlanta. ''When I called Delta,'' she told Atlanta personnel, ''Mr. Dean made arrangements for my son to be placed on the first flight out of Atlanta to Boston. Mr. Dean then called my son at his apartment to notify him of the flight departure. Mr. Dean then called me to personally offer my son the use of his own car to drive the 27 miles to Lawrence. Mr. Williams in Atlanta was waiting for my son at the airport and gave him royal treatment. . . . I can't find words to express myself, to really say how grateful we all are to these wonderful men and to Delta Air Lines. . . .''

Mr. Russ Robinson, of Springfield, Missouri, told Delta, ''I don't know if you give recognition to Delta employees who go above and beyond the call of duty, but I feel that your Mr. Marvin Davenport should at least be commended or recognized in some way for the trust and human compassion he displayed. I wasn't aware that there were such individuals still on the face of the earth. . . . Rest assured that because of his action, Delta Air Lines has gained a very faithful follower and I will utilize your service every chance I have. . . .''

J. K. Engstrom, a pilot for one of Delta's major competitors, wrote an unusual tribute. He said, ''I am married to a Delta stewardess. Suddenly she suffered serious illness. I am familiar with the airline industry, but I have never witnessed greater courtesy and more genuine concern than was evidenced by Delta employees, both in Houston and Chicago. I would like to recognize everyone by name, but to do so would be to name every Delta employee with whom I have come in contact since Pat was hospitalized. . . . You have a corporate 'family' much to be envied, and I for one, am most proud to have a wife who is a part of it. . . .''

People do make the difference. There are fund drives to help in many ways. Last year, systemwide personnel saved coupons and raised money to buy a kidney machine to save a desperately ill child; raised money to support Christian City, a children's home; and even raised funds to help individual families. Unfortunately, the whole list of these accomplishments is too lengthy to publish, but it is one filled with examples which seldom make front page news, but which, taken as a whole, make life a pleasant experience.

Perhaps the strongest bond (and here might lie the true secret of Delta) is that which exists between the employees themselves. "I know," a Delta supervisor said, "that when I ask a fellow employee to assume a responsibility for me that I don't have to ask twice. I take for granted the job will be done well, and go on to other projects. I'm in safe hands all the way. I do the same things for them many times every day. If someone asks me to do something, I get it done even if it means working late hours. I expect it of them and they expect it of me. In short, we have great faith and unlimited trust in each other. In addition, we have the world's finest airline management group behind all of us. They back us to the hilt. It's nice to be able to work in such an environment of pleasure and confidence. Would you believe that we look forward to every day at Delta?"

The Delta bond goes beyond even that. Delta people appear to have a warm feeling for each other, one most unusual in modern times. Consider Charles Walker, an aircraft overhaul foreman. Walker's wife had suffered serious illness. Hospital bills had mounted speedily, to over $16,000. "Never was Delta's group insurance so appreciated," Walker told company executives. "But even with the insurance there were still heavy expenses. My house needed immediate and costly repairs. The roof had begun to go. Word got around the company. Suddenly one morning a group of employees showed up for 'roofing duty.' They bought all the materials and re-roofed my house! Lunch was served to the 'roofers' by employee wives. The job was completed in one day. It was a wonderful surprise."

Computer Operator Wendell Hammett's eight-year-old son was badly burned. Employees donated blood and dollars to help. Toys were taken to the boy to occupy him during his confinement at the hospital. Babysitters stayed around the clock. "It was a heartening experience which I will never forget," Hammett said.

Silas Wumbush, a stores utility employee, received massive burns and his house was destroyed when a hot water heater exploded. Fellow employees donated money, clothing, and furniture. They completely equipped a new house and clothed the Wumbush family. No questions were asked and no thanks were really expected.

Dan Bough, a supervisor, had terminal cancer. During his confinement over several years, employees fought the battle with Mr. Bough because, as they said, "It's our fight too. He's one of us, isn't he?" Employees, tireless in their care, paid for the return of his son and the son's family from France where the young man served as a missionary. The son later wrote his father's fellow employees, "What you have been doing all along has been greater than anything I've ever heard of. The reputation of Delta goes far beyond all of that which is known to the public. None of it can be forgotten. Thank you all so much. . . ."

The list of good works by Delta's people goes on, inspiring, endless.

Delta is a modern, highly technical organization which appears to have met the challenge of today's difficult world head on and won. For it is a corporation with heart—28,000 people working together, pulling together, to make a heritage come true and stay alive. Delta people, as they tell the public repeatedly, are "Ready When You Are!"

STANLEY G. KARSON

Stanley G. Karson, Director of the Clearinghouse on Corporate Social Responsibility, heads the industry-wide effort begun early in 1972 by four associations of the nation's life and health insurance companies. The purpose of the Clearinghouse is to provide information and guidance to 450 insurance companies on corporate social responsibility activities and issues.

Born in New York, Mr. Karson graduated from Harvard College and received his Master's Degree in Political Science at the Harvard Graduate School of Public Administration. He was legislative assistant to U.S. Senator Herbert H. Lehman of New York for six years, then became an aide to Adlai E. Stevenson in his 1956 presidential campaign.

Late in 1957 he joined the Washington office of the Institute of Life Insurance. In 1966 he moved to the New York headquarters of the Institute to take the position of Director of Communications. In that capacity his primary responsibility came to involve the relationship of the business to social, urban, and community problems. He was involved in the formation of the National Urban Coalition in 1967 and served as chairman of the 1969 Life Insurance Company Urban Affairs Conference at Airlie House in Virginia.

He served as staff assistant to the Steering Committee of chief executive officers of the life and health insurance business and to the Conference on Corporate Social Responsibility convoked by the Steering Committee in October, 1971. When the Clearinghouse evolved from this meeting, he was appointed director in January, 1972. He has spoken at a number of conferences on corporate social responsibility.

Chapter 3

More Than Just Policies and Premiums

STANLEY G. KARSON

The chief executive officer of one of the major insurance companies recently said, "I'm not concerned that 10 years from now this business will look back on its social responsibility activities and conclude that we've done too much. My fear is that we'll know then that we've done too little."

This view is shared by many in the life and health insurance business. It stems from an understandable combination of concern, commitment, and pragmatism.

The life and health insurers, and particularly the former because of their longer tradition of serving the security needs of millions of American families, have tended for the most part to look upon their business as a social institution. None of them denies the importance of profits and of a successful business operation; on the other hand, more than many other types of business they have seen themselves as bound up intrinsically with the people's economic needs. Whether or not this is rationalization or reality is not important. It is felt strongly by many who have spent most of their lives in the life insurance business, and it has had a substantial impact on their view of corporate social responsibility.

Life insurance companies have been more willing than some others to place themselves in a leadership position in this area for another reason. They have been on the national or regional scene for generations, some for over a century, and a distinct relationship has grown between the companies and their communities.

Few other businesses—with the banks being a possible exception—occupy such a pervasive position in hundreds of communities throughout the country. The life insurance business, through its home offices, regional or field offices, or its agents, is present throughout our society.

Life insurance spokesmen, particularly over the past few years, have said many times that their companies are necessarily involved with the social and economic well-being of their communities. Their home and regional offices are located for the most part in the cities; their policy-holders live there; and the investments of the companies are to be found largely there.

This concern has led life insurance companies to demonstrate their social responsibilities on two complementary levels. Although the life insurance business, with its many hundreds of companies, is a highly competitive one, its self-image as a social institution of long standing has made it uniquely susceptible to industry-wide efforts involving social responsibility activities.

At the same time, many individual companies have developed their own community programs. A number of them can be traced back to the days when the term "corporate social responsibility" was unknown, and many business leaders could not justify involving their corporations in any substantial effort that did not boost the proverbial "bottom line."

COMPANY PROJECTS

Metropolitan Life's public health information and education programs were begun in the early years of this century. One important consequence of these programs was the development of the visiting nurse service. In more recent years, Metropolitan, like many of its counterparts in the business, has become aware of more specific social needs, and since the 1960's the minority community with its backlog of unmet needs has received particular attention.

In mid-1970, the School of Public Health and Administrative Medicine of the Faculty of Medicine, Columbia University, through its program of Continuing Education, approached Metropolitan Life for financial assistance to support several activities to improve health services in the inner city. These officials were strongly committed to the idea that good health service in these areas is a major factor in changing patterns of existing frustration and inability to achieve the most ordinary goals.

Metropolitan Life was especially interested in assisting the development of a new approach to health care for the Harlem community. The request for assistance in developing this new approach was reviewed by members of the staffs at Metropolitan's Department of Health and Welfare and the Department of Urban Affairs.

Staff analysis indicated that one of the greatest areas of concern in the ghetto hospital was the emergency room. Without exception, such facilities were overcrowded and understaffed. It was estimated that the emergency room at Harlem Hospital attended to more than

400 people a day. Often, whatever care was given at that time was the only medical attention the patient ever received.

If a more complete history were taken and diagnostic testing done on admittance to the emergency room, a system of referral could be established, and signs of illness, in addition to the malady which had brought the patient in on an emergency basis, could be detected. The patient could then receive subsequent treatment in the outpatient clinic or whatever unit seemed necessary.

It was apparent that history-taking and basic testing could be performed by a well-trained medical assistant. A training program could provide a group of assistants to help the nurses and physicians perform standard emergency procedures and enable them to see more patients more quickly.

A course was designed for four months' duration, with students to undergo three phases of training: (1) human relations in a hospital setting, (2) practical courses of study with on-the-job training, and (3) evaluation.

Metropolitan Life approved the request for support of this program and made a grant of $28,000, as a one-time contribution, in order to get the program started. Its letter of transmittal pointed out that the company had a long history of supporting demonstration projects in various public health areas, and that it had been found advisable for Metropolitan representatives to be able to observe the progress of the projects. Periodic reports of progress and a complete report and evaluation upon its conclusion were requested.

Considerable time was devoted to formulating the curriculum and program. Throughout this period, it became evident that the curriculum described at the time of the initial proposal provided insufficient training and skill and that what was needed were highly skilled individuals who could function as a physician's "right hand."

A true upgrading approach was stressed so that a candidate could ultimately attain any position in the present medical heirarchy, including physician or specialist. To attain this goal would, of course, require academic recognition and accreditation. This aim for high standards was thoroughly reinforced when the interviewers began conferring with potential trainee candidates and found high professional aspirations among these persons. Further, when the plan was discussed with officials of the New York City Health and Hospital Corporation, they counseled that focusing should be on permanent Physician Associate job titles rather than lower categories of employment.

Seven agencies became involved in the project after Metropolitan's grant was made. Their involvement resulted in the sharing of expertise, counseling, and funding, with the largest grant coming from the National Institutes of Health. Others participating were:

Antioch College, Washington-Baltimore Campus; District Council 37, American Federation of State, County and Municipal Employees, a major union within the municipal hospital system; Manpower Career Development Administration, Human Resources Administration, City of New York; New York City Health and Hospital Corporation; Harlem Hospital Center; and Columbia University, School of Public Health, Program of Continuing Education.

The program's objectives are:
a. To act as a community center.
b. To educate the community in the techniques of preventive medicine by providing training in prenatal care, hygiene, etc.
c. To provide an opportunity for community residents to be educated as allied medical professionals, community workers, health aides, etc.
d. To be a center for the community's education of health professionals and lay workers.
e. To be a center of community pride—a living, changing example of what members of the community, working together, can achieve.

Students enrolled initially in the program included neighborhood residents, persons already on the hospital staffs in lesser career jobs and Vietnam veterans.

The project is now known as Antioch College—Harlem Hospital Center. Graduates will be awarded certificates as Physician Associates through the New York State Department of Education and a Bachelor of Science Degree from Antioch College.

The original class of 10 received their degrees in December, 1973, and was followed by a second class of 20 students. Plans for a third class of 30 to begin in 1974 have been formulated. Over 300 applications have been received from prospective applicants. Remedial academic work for the students is being provided by Harlem Preparatory School, an institution to which Metropolitan Life has made substantial contributions over a long period.

No one who has lived in this country in the past 10 or 20 years can be oblivious to the adverse effects of inadequate educational opportunities in our society. When, in 1964, The Equitable Life Assurance Society voluntarily signed the Federal Government's Plans for Progress program, the company became involved in a special program, under the Progress umbrella, to enhance educational opportunities. The program was called the "Living Witness" project. Black executives in companies were asked to lecture at black colleges and universities, emphasizing the message that all fields of endeavor were now open to black students. The objective was to encourage black students to think of career opportunities beyond those in education or religion, which had traditionally been pursued.

Equitable's Chairman, James F. Oates, Jr., asked Joseph Farrar, then in Equitable's Law Department, to participate in 1965 as a "Living Witness" at Wiley College in Marshall, Texas. At that school Mr. Farrar addressed the whole student body in an assembly and consulted many students on career education in separate interviews. For many of the students, especially those from rural backgrounds, he was the first black lawyer they had ever seen.

In 1967, a manager from Equitable's Personnel Department, and a few other black executives representing other corporations in the area, became disenchanted with the lack of support from Washington for the Living Witness program. With the assistance of the National Alliance of Businessmen, a New York City Task Force on Youth Motivation was formed. Qualifications for Living Witnesses were changed to include not only professionals but also high school graduate employees from inner cities.

From 1967 to 1970, Equitable had approximately 15 to 20 Living Witnesses who made an average of three visits annually to high schools in New York City. Interest appeared to fade as a result of inadequate coordination and leadership; in 1971–1972 there were only 10 Living Witnesses at Equitable.

In January, 1973, Farrar, then Urban Affairs Director, launched a crash recruitment drive, resulting in an additional 24 employee volunteers for the program. Employees were selected from lower grades for the first time. Not only were younger employees to be represented but also students were to find it easier to relate to these representatives of business.

In the 1973–1974 school year, 10 visits to New York City junior and senior high schools were scheduled.

Since 1972, Equitable has been involved with a youth motivation project at the Clinton Annex, a junior high school at 54th Street and 8th Avenue in Manhattan, which adopted the "open walls" concept of education. Students take their classes in the school in the morning and venture out to different corporations in the afternoon for elective classes.

Last year Equitable assisted the school in an audiovisual class held at the company studio. Equitable's role will be broadened somewhat by participating in a video exchange program to be patterned after one previously carried out with considerable success by Benjamin Franklin Preparatory School and Rye, New York, Country Day School students. This will involve a series of exchanges of videotapes between Clinton students and a selected group of eight Living Witnesses.

The selected witnesses have already videotaped 90 minutes of discussion that includes topics such as punctuality, attitudes, behavior, job satisfaction, and life styles of young employees. The tape is realistic and alive. The group will be convened for a last editing session to obtain the best 30 minutes possible for purposes of the exchange.

The Living Witness approach has proven to be educational for both students and employees. The employee has an opportunity to compare the present climate in city schools with his own years in school. In most instances, it is an eye-opening experience. The students, in turn, are made to feel that someone cares.

At present, a black employee in Equitable Group Operations serves as Manhattan coordinator for the New York City Task Force on Youth Motivation (Living Witness), while Mr. Farrar coordinates Equitable's participation. Now in its ninth year, Equitable's involvement in the Living Witness activity represents a transition from compliance participation at the outset, to a period of benign neglect, to the present intensive programming, which finds the activity an increasingly significant part of the way Equitable goes about its business.

Another company, Connecticut Mutual Life in Hartford, was able to help both an individual and a community through financial as well as technical assistance.

In 1971 Joel Gordon had a dream. The recently appointed manager of the Stowe Village public housing development in Hartford's North End wanted to see a co-op store established as part of his five-year plan to rejuvenate the low-income housing project.

The Hartford Housing Authority agreed to let a co-op group take over an empty apartment for the venture, and Gordon turned to Connecticut Mutual Life, a company he had worked with previously while a City Parks and Recreation Department employee, to get resource people to help with the store.

The store was opened with due ceremonies in September, 1971, with the mayor and other dignitaries present. Within two weeks, however, the store had $700 in inventory and $3,000 in outstanding debts to vendors. It was necessary to close its doors.

"We stopped everything and stepped back to take a long hard look at what was happening," explained Frank Keitt of the Knox Foundation, one of the agencies that had cooperated in the birth of the store. "Then we sat down with some community residents and some experts in the field to see how we could get this thing moving again."

Thomas Truglio and Robert Andrews from Connecticut Mutual were among the experts called in. It was concluded that the store immediately needed detailed procedures for operating, four full-time competent workers, and $2,400 in working capital.

Acting strictly on faith—a belief in the dedication and honesty of the community residents involved—Connecticut Mutual agreed to loan the store $500. The Knox Foundation provided another $400, and the balance was obtained from the Small Business Development Corporation.

The entire $2,400 loan was repaid only five months after the Stowe Village Co-op once again opened its doors to business with a new and properly trained manager and staff. The store grossed $105,000 in sales in 1972, and total sales in 1973 were estimated to hit $160,000, according to Connecticut Mutual personnel who have watched and assisted the store's growth.

One of the more recent examples of individual company activity comes from Equitable Life Insurance Company of Iowa.

In September, 1973, the company invited the Volunteer Bureau of Des Moines to help conduct a Volunteer Fair in its home office. The Bureau represents 128 agencies. To run the Fair, they were divided into 13 categories, each being represented by a Bureau member with the assistance of one of Equitable's employees. All company personnel were invited to visit the displays on a scheduled basis so that they would have ample time to learn about any agencies in which they might have a particular interest.

At the end of the Volunteer Fair, more than 40 employees—some 10 per cent of the home office staff—had expressed an interest in performing volunteer work on their own time. A month later, 22 of these persons were actually performing such work, and arrangements were pending for a number of others. The community's Volunteer Bureau regarded this effort as quite successful, and many of Equitable's employees expressed appreciation for the opportunity to learn more about the social programs which exist in their community.

The story of one volunteer and the service which she is performing as a result of this program is cited by Equitable of Iowa as an example of the unexpected and gratifying results which can come from efforts to involve the corporation and its employees in social problems.

Miss L. has been an employee of the company less than one year. She is a member of a minority group and attended high school, like many young people, mainly because of parental pressure. Although she received her high school diploma she indicated no interest in further education.

Through the Volunteer Fair, Miss L. volunteered to work at the Fort Des Moines Correctional Facility. The purpose of this unique residential facility is to educate, counsel, and seek employment for men who have been charged with felonies. They are permitted to hold jobs in the community during their stay.

Miss L. spent three evenings each week, from 7 to 10 P.M., serving as a tutor, working mainly with two men. Most tutoring is at the very basic level of education, for some men at the Center cannot tell time or count change, and some do not even recognize the letters of the alphabet. Miss L. feels that the most important talents for a tutor are being patient and being a good listener.

Although there were some who doubted her ability in this area at the outset, supervisors reported that Miss L. has made a genuine contribution. She offered a number of very constructive suggestions to improve the Facility's program, and she became actively engaged in recruiting others to join in her work.

Still another company, Security Life and Accident Company of Denver, became involved in a significant social activity which was conceived, created, and is now being implemented by its employees.

The group invited representatives of four Denver area organizations to appear before Security Life's employee Task Force to acquaint participants with available projects. From these presentations, the Task Force selected a project designated "Employ-eX." This is an undertaking funded and originated through the Law Enforcement Assistance Administration (LEAA) as one of that national agency's programs directed toward reduction of high impact crimes.

Employ-eX was created and is administered by ex-law offenders who have been incarcerated in penal institutions. Realizing that most individuals in prison and other penal institutions are repeat offenders, this group hoped to weaken the vicious circle of the repeat offenders by offering redirection, motivation, and reemployment. Their primary aim has been to develop jobs for ex-offenders and to assist them in finding job success by causing attitude changes and offering moral and psychological back-up. The Denver staff of Employ-eX includes four ex-offenders. They are finding jobs for approximately 15 former convicts each month.

As with most socially oriented projects, Employ-eX lacks sufficient funds for adequate staffing. Consequently, Security Life Task Force members help to fill staffing requirements which could not otherwise be met. Since the company is on a four-day work week, one or more Task Force members are available each week to assist in the Employ-eX office.

In addition, members of the Task Force have become involved in food and clothing drives to assist the ex-offender and his family during the period between discharge and employment. Recently the group negotiated for a centrally located empty building which will be made available by the owners to the Employ-eX organization rent free for 12 months in order to set up a clothing bank. Task Force members also regularly participate in orientation and training sessions with groups of just-released prisoners. These classes are designed to assist the ex-offender, psychologically and otherwise, to most effectively apply for employment. Teaching techniques range from lectures to mock interviews.

On several occasions, Task Force members have been successful in securing job interviews, and even employment, for released prisoners. Task Force members have also visited and delivered Christmas gifts to the Colorado Pre-Parole Center. Other contacts with prisoners prior to release are contemplated, including orientation classes at the Center.

As one Security Life employee, who participated in the Task Force from its inception, put it:

Our involvement can only be felt and shown and is difficult to express on paper. This is something very real, not just a well-meant but nonproductive discussion held during a coffee break. We believe we are reaching out just a little bit to people less fortunate than we.

Those of us who have met with these people on frequent occasions, and tried to provide them with a new insight into society, have found that we aren't nearly so far apart as we might have imagined. We know we are helping many of the former offenders to make a new and productive life for themselves.

The Task Force established an initial annual budget of $850 which is used for direct assistance to Employ-eX. The company contributes $200 of this amount. The rest comes from the employees who are members of the Involvement Corps Task Force, and from fund raising activities mounted by the Task Force. In addition, the company makes an annual contribution of $1,800 to the Involvement Corps. Pledges (averaging $100 a month) by Task Force members also support the Involvement Corps.

Security Life is proud of this movement. Some time ago the company adopted as its corporate philosophy "Commitment to Excellence." The employee Task Force has enlarged this concept and adopted as its personal goal: "Commitment to Care."

Six Hartford-based insurers—Aetna Life & Casualty, Connecticut General, Connecticut Mutual, Hartford Insurance Group, Phoenix Mutual, and Travelers—are among some 30 companies that have spearheaded the Greater Hartford Process, an unprecedented attack on the complexities of urban breakdown.

Greater Hartford Process was born out of the realization that a long succession of past efforts hadn't done the job. Hartford business had been involved in one big push after another, trying to check the decline of urban neighborhoods and institutions. In the late 1960's, it began a search for solutions by creating Greater Hartford Corporation, a non-profit group composed of executives from contributing companies.

This new organization in turn hired the American City Corporation, brainchild of James Rouse, whose success with the new city of Columbia, Maryland, was already offering new possibilities for urban living. Out of the Rouse group's two-year study of the community came the Greater Hartford Process, a formula for community action.

Process started with the assumption that one way or another— with good planning or without it—$2 billion to $3 billion would be spent in the 1970's in Greater Hartford for homes, shopping centers, factories, offices, schools, streets, municipal buildings, and other capital development to support population growth estimated in the hundreds of thousands.

Without good planning on a metropolitan level, this huge investment would have the same chaotic effect on the area and its environment that had been experienced previously. Vast acreage would be consumed by ill-conceived residential subdivisions; traffic jams would get worse; gaudy strip zoning along the main thoroughfares would proliferate; the suffering of the poor in the inner city would grow more intense; and de facto racial segregation would intensify as the inner city grew "blacker" and the suburbs grew "whiter."

Greater Hartford Process was conceived as the way citizens could plan to avoid these problems, decide what kind of community they wanted to live in, and how they could make it happen.

To support this citizen effort, Greater Hartford Corporation created Process, Inc., a planning and implementing unit, and Devco, a physical development unit which assures that the community will have the capacity to follow through on its physical renewal plans.

Reflecting the need to make Process, Inc., responsive to the people, its board of directors was created to include representatives of all segments of the community—the poor, the blacks, women, Puerto Ricans, city government, suburban government, social service agencies, labor, business, and others.

The companion company of Process, Inc., Devco, was deliberately organized as a specialized business operation whose board includes experts in finance, construction, and land development.

As the development arm of Process, Devco can undertake no development project without the approval of the Process board. But Devco has the right to refuse any development proposal by Process, Inc., which it deems to be an unsound business undertaking.

In some cases, Devco will itself be a community developer. In other cases it will help private groups and municipal agencies to find other suitable developers.

In May, 1972, Process released a report for community discussion which contained new ideas for education, social services, housing, police, mass transportation, medical services, and other life support systems essential to a good working community.

The report spells out the virtues of building total new suburban communities on a scale of at least 1,000 acres for populations of 10,000 or more. It proposes that these communities include young people, old people, minority groups, people in several income groups, people with varying educational backgrounds, and of course, a mixture of single and multi-family housing to support the needs of this diverse population.

The report also proposes an $800 million redevelopment effort in an area covering 40 per cent of the city of Hartford, including its central business district and major concentration of low income neighborhoods.

When it was released, the report promptly came under sharp criticism from some areas of the community. Much of the criticism did not actually deal with the proposals themselves but centered instead on distrust of "the establishment" and the motives of business in backing this effort.

In the late 1960's, as the groundwork for the Greater Hartford Process was being laid, a feeling of futility was sensed through the community. Many people had ideas for solving this problem or that problem, but few believed it was possible to turn their ideas into action. The urban-suburban scene was just too complicated — or so went the conventional wisdom.

The main goal of Process's report, with all its ambitious proposals, has been to demonstrate that there are ways to achieve a better quality of life for all citizens.

Citizens may decide to reject some proposals in favor of better ones. This is all part of Process, Inc. It makes choices among solutions, but it rejects the old habit of making no decision at all.

Actually, the Process is already said to have profound impact on community decision making. New kinds of decisions and actions are occurring in many segments of the community.

Community leaders approach major decisions today with greater consciousness of the effect of those decisions on other aspects of community life. Increasingly, the staff of Process, Inc., and Devco are being consulted for help and ideas. All this is a source of great encouragement for the sponsors and architects of this vast effort. It's what they spent millions of dollars and untold amounts of personal energy to try to get started.

Allstate Insurance Companies decided to look to its own areas of experience and special interest when seeking worthwhile and effective ways in which to help meet the urban crisis.

One successful example of this philosophy has been an auto body repair skill training center which Allstate established in mid-1973 in Chicago's blighted South Side under the sponsorship of

Opportunities Industrialization Centers, Inc. (OIC), the nation's largest private, non-profit manpower training organization.

OIC was established in 1964 in Philadelphia by Dr. Leon Sullivan, a Baptist minister. The first organization was started in an abandoned jail with $10 apiece from 400 of Dr. Sullivan's parishioners. OIC now has programs in some 100 American cities.

Allstate suggested to OIC that the ground floor of an empty bottling plant donated to OIC by Coca-Cola be used to set up an auto body repair skill training center. "This was a field with which we were familiar and could contribute our own expertise, and we knew there is a shortage of trained auto body repair men," explained Jack Walgren, Urban Affairs Director for Allstate Insurance Companies.

Considerable remodeling of the former bottling plant was necessary for the new use. Allstate obtained local bids for the remodeling and selected a contractor from the immediate area, an economically depressed black neighborhood.

Allstate's commitment to meeting the start-up costs for the training center's first year of operation included purchasing the variety of tools and equipment needed for the project, with some tools being donated by manufacturers. The largest single item was a spray paint booth which included a compressed air system.

Allstate also established the center's technical curriculum, produced training manuals and student workbooks, and lent a skilled instructor for the center's first year. The company donated salvage automobiles for instructional repair work, turning the titles over to OIC. When repaired, the cars were resold by OIC, with the revenue helping to meet the cost of maintenance supplies.

OIC's role has been to recruit and motivate the students for the training center. With few exceptions they are young men, many of them Vietnam veterans, who lack a valuable skill and are unemployed or underemployed. There is no charge for the six-month auto body repair training course.

The company points out that it regards meaningful employment as a crucial element in the fight to overcome our urban crises. To help its graduates get jobs, the training center lends them the $200 they need to buy a complete set of tools. And in time, when they have accumulated enough experience and capital, these men can look forward to opening their own body repair shops.

The Chicago training center has proved so successful that Allstate and OIC have planned a similar facility in 1973 in Atlanta. Allstate and OIC had planned to open two more auto body repair training centers by the end of 1973, one in northern New Jersey and the other in the San Francisco area. Mr. Walgren has said:

As each of these centers becomes established and productive, we look to the local community to take over its support, possibly with the use of revenue sharing funds. We feel this kind of job training program is an excellent example of how business and industry can join with responsible social organizations and concerned citizens in finding realistic solutions to the problems of our times.

The Prudential Insurance Company of America, under the direction of its two most recent chairmen, Orville E. Beal and Donald S. MacNaughton, has become increasingly involved in the myriad problems of its home office city of Newark, New Jersey. Whether through investments, contributions or the loan of officers to the city government, Prudential has made clear its corporate concern for Newark.

As the country's largest life insurance company, Prudential's social responsibility activities cover many communities. Minneapolis provides just one example:

Charlie Johnson was trained as an electrician by the U.S. Navy. When he was discharged in 1959, the future looked bright: he was young and he was skilled. The problem was that he was also black—a fact which did not enhance his candidacy for a union apprenticeship.

And so, for the next nine years, Charlie Johnson, electrician, became Charlie Johnson, janitor (at $65 a week) and later Charlie Johnson, assistant baker (at $90 a week). The open horizon had turned into a dead-end street.

In 1973, four years after the baker's job, he was taking home up to 50 per cent more pay as a senior test technician at a Control Data Corporation manufacturing plant in the black community of North Minneapolis.

Charlie Johnson is now in his late thirties. For the first time since his Navy days, he feels he has a future.

As the Minneapolis Tribune put it in a 2,500-word illustrated feature spread across eight columns of its business page, it was the Charlie Johnsons of this imperfect world who led Control Data (CDC) into the black community of Minneapolis nearly five years before in an experiment designed to take jobs to the people of low-income areas.

The project, financed in part by Prudential as a commitment under the industry's Urban Investment Program, has been cited as one of the more successful ventures to train minority group members and place them in productive jobs.

The record shows nearly 850 jobs for low-income minority members and whites at CDC's four plants, including 500 in the black community's Northside plant. Also created were part-time jobs, many of them filled by welfare mothers and students, at the company's bindery plant in St. Paul's Selby-Dale area.

The record also shows an annual payroll of nearly $4.5 million.

The Prudential participated through a $4 million purchase of a training school and plant which were subsequently leased to CDC. In addition to providing jobs for black construction workers, the company's financial involvement resulted in 270 permanent new jobs.

The success story, however, is perhaps told best by individuals rather than by statistics.

For Charlie Johnson and his wife and two children, his job has provided a home and the means to fix it up the way they want it.

And it has meant one thing more. As Mr. Johnson put it: "I can tell people I've got a respectable job now—that I'm not just scrubbing floors."

Finally, as an example of company concern about urban problems, New York Life Insurance Company has carved out its own significant role.

The task of evaluating and coordinating the many facets of its urban program belongs to the company's Urban Activities Committee and Urban Investment Committee, whose members include investment, mortgage loan, marketing, personnel, public relations and corporate responsibility officers.

The Urban Activities Committee is charged with the responsibility of making the best use of the company's contributions to agencies dealing with problems of the inner city. For example, New York Life has been aiding a health screening program in a section of the economically deprived South Bronx and was particularly pleased that its financial contribution triggered a substantial Model Cities grant. This is an example of the kind of effective leverage a company may achieve with its contribution dollars.

Its Urban Investment Committee, whose membership partly overlaps that of the other committee, seeks investment opportunities and medical and community services for some of the millions who are trapped in urban ghettos.

The activities of both committees represent the urban program which New York Life continued on its own after fulfilling its quota of $125 million in the life insurance industry's completed $2 Billion Urban Investment Program.

Over the past six years, New York Life's urban housing loans have helped make possible more than 7,000 new dwelling units, primarily for moderate- and low-income families. Commercial loans for office buildings and retail stores have helped to create nearly 8,000 new jobs. And in nearly half of its urban loans, minority or biracial groups have been the borrowers.

Today, the company can point to a Neighborhood Health Center in the ghetto area of Nashville, to over 500 new garden apartments for minority families in Houston, to a new day-care center in Brooklyn, and to shopping centers in the inner cities of Kansas City, Houston, and Chicago.

These examples of company activity can be multiplied many times throughout the business to indicate the extent of such efforts to come to grips with community needs. And it has obviously not been only the larger companies with the greatest financial resources which have become so involved. Companies of all sizes and individual officers and employees in every section of the country have begun a number of effective, often innovative, programs to meet social and economic needs.

INDUSTRY-WIDE PROGRAMS

Although a variety of company activities were directed to these problems over the years, the age of contemporary social responsibility did not emerge until the 1960's. During that decade, a new national awareness of the real significance and dimensions of social problems became apparent. This realization was nourished by the social upheavals of the period, and business, particularly the insurance business, was not to be excluded as a participant in the pursuit of national goals to alleviate basic social and economic problems.

Exposed for the first time, as were many Americans, to the true magnitude and significance of the plight of the disadvantaged, the minority groups, or the urban areas in general, leaders of the life insurance business on an industry level began in the mid-1960's to hold high level discussions about these problems and their relationship to them. Early in 1967 one of the major associations of life insurance companies voted to ask two other trade associations within the business to join in an attempt to devise some program which would permit the resources of the business to be brought to bear in some significant fashion upon the problems of the cities.

In midsummer, 1967, a Committee on Urban Problems, composed of chief executive officers of leading life insurance companies, decided to ask the companies to agree to commit a portion of their investments for housing and job opportunities in the cities. After receiving the assurance of enough companies that they would indeed commit sufficient funds for these purposes, leaders of the business arranged a meeting with President Lyndon B. Johnson to make the announcement.

On September 13, 1967, in the presence of Cabinet and Congressional leaders as well as representatives of urban-oriented and minority organizations, life insurance spokesmen announced the new program to the President. They stated that the participating life insurance companies had pledged a total of $1 billion for investments in low- and moderate-income housing for residents of city core areas and to finance job-creating enterprises and community facilities for residents of these areas. The yield on such investments was to be no higher than the normal interest rates of the individual company making the loan. This was to be the case even though these investments were to be in areas where no measurable capital had been invested by the public or private sectors for these purposes in years and although they were considered to be more than normal risks.

The Billion Dollar Program became the $2 Billion Dollar Program in April, 1969, when it was renewed, with a pledge to President Richard M. Nixon that more emphasis would be placed on investments in job-creating enterprises. The program was announced as completed in September, 1972, and the final figures are shown in Table 3–1.

A comprehensive evaluation of the entire program and its accomplishments and problems was made by the life insurance business under the supervision of a group of four urban experts led by Paul N. Ylvisaker, Dean of the Graduate School of Education at Harvard, who had served as the first Commissioner of Community Affairs of New Jersey during the late 1960's.

In order to evaluate its continuing role in the field of social and community involvement, representatives of the life insurance business in the fall of 1971 met for an unprecedented conference of 100 chief executives of life and health insurance companies on the subject of corporate social responsibility. Prudential's chairman, Mr.

TABLE 3–1   URBAN INVESTMENT PROGRAM OF THE
LIFE INSURANCE BUSINESS
Investments
(Status as of April 1, 1973)

	DOLLARS COMMITTED OR DISBURSED	
Housing		
Mortgages and Real Estate	$1,321,167,000	
Securities	24,816,000	
Total Housing*		$1,345,983,000
Job-Creating and Service Facilities		
Medical and Social Services	419,316,700	
Commercial and Industrial	270,354,000	
Minority Financial Institutions Deposits	7,295,000	
Total Job-Creating and Service Facilities		696,965,700
Grand Total		$2,042,948,700

*This figure accounts for 116,333 housing units.

MacNaughton, in his keynote cautioned his associates with this significant statement:

It was not God, but the people, who granted us permission to function, and not for our benefit, but for the public's—by the people and for the people. Only when we truly reach this understanding can we cast a clear focus on our rights and duties.

The primary purpose of the two-day conference was to establish at the highest level the philosophical foundation for the involvement of the business. Ad hoc approaches to it had perhaps been necessary in the past. But, if there was to be any permanent commitment by the business it was time to sit down, undisturbed, agree on basic principles and decide where to go.

The one clearly expressed consensus of the conference was the need for an industry-wide mechanism to provide companies and their officers and staffs with helpful information so that they might proceed to implement more effective programs in the various areas of corporate social responsibility. They wanted to know what other insurance companies were doing, how they were doing it, and where were the problems.

Out of this expressed need came the Clearinghouse on Corporate Social Responsibility created by the actions of the boards of four major life and health insurance associations in the winter of 1971–1972. It was to be a function of the Institute of Life Insurance, but reporting to an industry-wide Committee on Corporate Social Responsibility composed of 12 company chief executive officers representing the various associations. Six areas of major concern were set forth by the Clearinghouse for the 440 life and health insurance companies affiliated with it. These were:

1. Socially desirable investments, defined broadly as those which a company might not make in the normal course of its investment operations and were being made primarily for the social purposes involved.
2. Corporate contributions.
3. Community projects.
4. Individual involvement, or company encouragement of involvement by officers and other employees in community or governmental programs.
5. Employment and promotion practices involving women and members of minority groups.
6. The impact of the companies and their operations on the environment.

A Clearinghouse survey was conducted early in 1972 on company activities in these six areas. A few months later, the results of the survey for the industry as a whole were published and provided to all interested parties, particularly to the companies. This survey was heralded as the first in the annals of American business by an independent publication in the field of corporate social responsibility.

To inform the business of what specific company projects and activities were being performed in these various areas, a publication called *Response* was sent primarily to company officers and staff beginning in April, 1972, on a bimonthly basis. (Some of the examples of company programs recounted above have been described in *Response*.) Its value to the program and its purposes were seen at the outset as more than just an exchange of information, important though that is. It enables companies to see what others like them can do. It encourages those that are innovative in their programs and those whose activities demonstrate genuine commitment.

Early in 1973 the Committee on Corporate Social Responsibility approved a proposal for a new and permanent industry-wide reporting program in corporate social responsibility activities. Companies are asked to participate by reporting activities in the six areas of corporate social responsibility for the previous year and plans for the current year. The Clearinghouse aggregates the statistics, including dollars invested and contributed, numbers of women and minority group members hired and promoted, manhours of company personnel loaned to community programs or working with them on a released-time basis, numbers and types of community projects undertaken and environmental policies effected. The first industry-wide totals were made available at the end of 1973 by the Clearinghouse and provided to all member companies and other interested parties.

CONCLUSIONS

The foregoing account about the insurance business is not intended to demonstrate conclusively that the life and health insurance companies are doing all they might in the field of corporate social responsibility. It does suggest, however, that enough leaders at both the company and institutional level have been able over the years, particularly in the recent past, to move this business into a leadership position within the private sector.

That no unanimity exists throughout these leadership levels on appropriate courses of action in this field is not disputed. But whatever differences exist now are directed toward specific proposals or emphasis, not upon the fundamental question of the need to be involved in corporate social responsibility programs.

Ten or 20 years from now the various programs described here may well be viewed as inadequate. Such a view in the 1980's would not be at all surprising considering the momentum of recent years.

As important as it is to tell the story of what business is doing to attack social and economic ills, the story must be *worth* the telling. Above all, it must be based upon genuine commitment.

Surely the business system as we know it today will be the ultimate victim if the public perceives that there is corporate indifference to the nation's problems.

ROBERT W. GALVIN

In 1970, the Electronic Industries Association awarded its Medal of Honor to Robert W. Galvin, Chairman and Chief Executive Officer of Motorola, Inc., for his outstanding contribution to the advancement of the electronics industry.

Galvin was also selected "Decision Maker of the Year" in 1973 by the Chicago Association of Commerce and Industry and the American Statistical Association.

Galvin, company chairman since 1964, has been contributing to the industry since 1944, when he permanently joined Motorola. In 1956, he was named President of the company.

He is currently a director of Harris Trust and Savings Bank, director and past president of the Electronic Industries Association, a director of Junior Achievement of Chicago, a trustee of the Illinois Institute of Technology and one of 12 fellows of the University of Notre Dame. He was also a member of the President's Commission on International Trade and Investment.

Galvin attended the University of Notre Dame and the University of Chicago, and holds honorary degrees from Quincy College and St. Ambrose College.

Chapter 4

Motorola, Inc., and Chicago's Industrial Skill Center

ROBERT W. GALVIN

INTRODUCTION

The Lawndale neighborhood of Chicago's west side is undergoing change. Lawndale's crumbling, abandoned buildings are marked with graffiti delineating the borders of rival gang territories. The affluent society which once found the neighborhood a social center has now abandoned Lawndale in favor of the suburbs.

At 2815 West 19th Street in Lawndale stands a building which was once a milking machine factory. Its owners had decided to leave the building, the neighborhood, and its inhabitants in favor of larger facilities.

It is a good solid building with plenty of value left in it. But in its abandoned state, it was a neighborhood eyesore, a liability. The Chicago Board of Education purchased and renovated the building and has transformed it once again into a major community facility.

The building now houses the Industrial Skill Center, a remarkable example of an unusual fusion of education and industry. The Center is a unique and Promethean experimental venture in occupational education.

The Industrial Skill Center came into being as a consequence of the Chicago Board of Education's efforts to provide alternatives to the traditional high school. It is designed to turn dropouts into productive citizens through occupational education.

Occupational training is different from vocational training in that the student is actually producing a good or service paid for by a sponsoring company. Vocational training is a survey-type of educa-

53

tion and an introduction to occupational education; however, it stops short of involving the participant in a genuine industrial setting in which he is actually manufacturing a product for sale in the future. The student of the Industrial Skill Center gains knowledge of the industry in which he is involved, but more importantly, he becomes acclimated to the average industrial work setting, familiarizing himself with norms and expectations. Philip A. Viso calls it "the first and only school to look at industrial education from industry's point of view."

THE PRINCIPAL

Philip A. Viso is the principal of the Industrial Skill Center and the man who saw a need for this type of education. He is a man who had a vision and has been able to see it realized.

For a number of years, Viso had been a teacher in a Chicago public school. He was disturbed by a number of things which he thought were wrong with the traditional high school system. Primarily, he saw a need for the system to give further assistance to a young person even after he leaves school.

Until the Industrial Skill Center concept came into being, when a student was unable or unwilling to continue his high school education, he was more or less forgotten by the school system. He was then sent to fend for himself in the labor market with few marketable skills and, frequently, even fewer inclinations toward the work which would be required of him.

Viso saw that this situation was failing to meet the needs of the dropout and of the company with which he would apply for employment. Industry, for the most part, had been reluctant to invest time and money in untrained applicants. Viso saw a need for a more directly work-oriented training center. So began his vision.

Working with a team put together by Chicago's school area "B" assistant superintendent, Julian Drayton, and the Educational Program Department under the direction of Evelyn Carlson, Viso evolved a concept which would hinge on two main points:

1. The academic curricula of the Industrial Skill Center would revolve around individualized learning packages which would segment the material of a specific course into smaller units which the student would complete, one at a time, at his own pace.
2. Industry of the Chicago area would be enlisted to participate in the program by establishing production shops at the school, providing equipment and work for the students as well as an instructor to supervise the company's operation and to pro-

vide instruction. The sponsoring company would pay the Chicago Board of Education for products and services received and the school, in turn, would pay the students.

THE INDUSTRIAL SKILL CENTER

The Chicago Board of Education responded enthusiastically to this concept. The purchase of the ex-factory building was arranged. In addition to the initial expenditure of $120,000 on the building, $100,000 was allocated for restoration of the building—lighting, painting, plumbing, heating, carpeting, and general clean-up.

The renovation was completed in late 1969, and occupancy of the Industrial Skill Center was begun with the September, 1969, term.

The building is divided into three main sections. The industrial shops are on the first floor of the building. In one section, operated by Western Electric, telephone cables are formed by the students; in the other section, operated by Motorola, Inc., students are taught basic electronics and how to test automobile parts for possible defects. On the second floor is a large, open learning center in which the students spend about 50 per cent of their time. It includes four study areas for science, mathematics, social studies, and English. In addition, there are intensive reading and math centers for students whose skills are below eighth-grade level in these areas.

Students attending the Industrial Skill Center represent nearly all steps on the socioeconomic ladder, from lower–lower class to upper middle class. The students possess some characteristics which are similar to each other and many which are widely divergent.

THE STUDENTS

The students attending the Industrial Skill Center are between the ages of 16 and 20, and have been out of school for three months to three years. In some instances, the student just disappeared from school. In other cases, administrators excluded them from school at the age of 16, citing their disruptive influence on the other students as the reason.

Philip Viso affectionately calls his students "mavericks," in the sense that they haven't conformed to traditional patterns of behavior, and they refuse to be forced to conform. Because they refuse to acquiesce to society's norms, according to Viso, there evolves a sub-society which frequently takes the form of street gangs or other groups whose existence can be maintained only through socially unacceptable means. Since they cannot succeed in the greater society, success in the gang becomes imperative, and this success is usually measured by aggressiveness. The main function of the Industrial Skill Center is to turn this aggressiveness into socially acceptable ends by using it as a tool in the education of the "maverick."

In many instances, traditional schools find it more expedient to repress this aggression than to utilize it. But Viso believes it is the natural aggressiveness of our society's leaders that has been a major factor in their success, and that there are ways of channeling their aggression into productive ends.

Another characteristic common to the dropout is alienation from his home, school, and community. This alienation often is manifested in acts of violence and vandalism perpetrated against these institutions. "A conservative estimate of 50 per cent of our students are known to the courts," says Viso. "Charges range from simple curfew violations to major felonies."

In a significant percentage of the Industrial Skill Center students, there is an inability to use time wisely. Students asked to appear at 9 A.M. often appear as late as 3 P.M., seemingly unable to comprehend time or to follow directions relating to place. These students represent two extremes in behavior—one being laziness and disinterest, the second representing the hyperactive, highly volatile response to directions. A typical example of this behavior is the student who is told that the Industrial Skill Center does not appear to be meeting his requirements, and that therefore he should find a program which better suits his needs. The student begs to be permitted to remain at the Industrial Skill Center, vowing never to miss a class again. When his promises are accepted, he promptly absents himself from school on that same day. When later confronted with this latest absence, he violently argues that there is a conspiracy among the faculty to have him dropped from the school. He seems unable to recognize his role in assisting himself to succeed.

Viso estimates that traditional schools, at best, serve the needs of about 60 per cent of those students who attend, due to a lack of opportunities for the creative, troubled, introverted and discontented student. The Industrial Skill Center offers a viable alternative to the traditional system by providing a two-fold solution to the problem: The student can gain knowledge of an industrial occupation while earning money, and he can complete the requirements for his high school diploma—at his own pace.

All new students entering the program spend one week in an orientation program conducted by the counseling office, and involving all members of the teaching staff as well as members of the administrative staff. During the orientation, the student is given the opportunity to learn what the school has to offer and who his fellow students are. The introductory week also provides the staff with an opportunity to get to know the student and learn about his strengths and weaknesses, his hopes and frustrations, family relationships and general outlook on life. This is done informally through "rap" sessions, at which the student is able to feel comfortable and willing to express himself.

After the week-long counseling session, the student is brought into the academic program of the school.

ACADEMIC CURRICULUM

It has been found by the Center's staff that a common reason for a student's failure to succeed in a traditional high school is an inability or an unwillingness to compete with his peers. A fear of failure and its resulting ridicule can be strong limitations on healthy competition. Upon seeing the need for a noncompetitive learning technique, the Center's faculty developed a series of individualized learning packages.

The packages basically are sections of traditional learning materials. They are standardized, in that all students must meet certain levels of proficiency before moving to new subjects, but they are at the same time individualized, since the student may work steadily toward prescribed goals at a speed which he finds acceptable.

Teachers lead discussions and administer tests to students upon completion of each section. The result of the exam is either "passing or incomplete." The student immediately understands that failure is impossible, that the only variable in his studies is the time involved for completion of the course. An "incomplete" means that the student must review the material until his level of proficiency meets accepted standards as measured by the tests. Instructors help the student with problem sections.

Viso says, "We have found that the reluctant learner becomes aggressive in his desire to learn if he knows where he is going and what the requirements are. With our method, each part of the instructional program becomes part of the requirements for graduation."

The individualized help required by this system means that the pupil/teacher ratio at the Center must necessarily be quite low. At the Industrial Skill Center, there is one instructor for every 20 students.

INSTRUCTORS

Development of this new style of education meant that a new breed of teacher had to be developed to meet the special needs of the unusual student body.

The teacher at the Center must be able to accept more unusual modes of behavior than in the average classroom situation. It was necessary that the instructor have the ability to generate personal concern and empathy with his students, to earn their respect, rather than feel that it was due him because of his status as teacher.

The teacher would have to look beyond the overt behavioral symptoms which, in many cases, take the form of maladaptive aggression, to search for root causes which, over the long run, could be resolved, thereby bringing about behavioral modification.

Teachers at the Industrial Skill Center are all accredited teachers. They were selected with great care, from numerous applicants, and then placed in an intensive in-service training program designed to enhance the basic attitudes and skills they brought with them. The program consists, in part, of sensitivity training at weekly meetings. The result of this training has been to unite the staff toward a common goal. Viso says, "The sensitivity training has taught us to work together and to understand the divergent philosophies we hold. Students participate in many of these sessions, providing us with further insight into the school's problems and building a bridge of trust and understanding between students, faculty and administrative staff."

It is Viso's belief that education must provide students with a marketable skill. "Traditional vocational education programs in the eyes of the students fail to do this," he said. "Training of a more specific nature with an identifiable occupation as a result must be the direction in which we work." It is for this reason that the Center's occupational education program was instituted.

OCCUPATIONAL EDUCATION

The Western Electric Shop

In 1970, Western Electric began operating a cable-forming assembly shop on the first floor of the Industrial Skill Center. In this shop, 40 students train for 20 hours a week. They receive wages of between $1.70 and $2.50 per hour, depending on their proficiency. During the training cycle, they produce cables at a rate which usually equals or exceeds that produced at Western Electric's Hawthorne plant.

The Motorola Shop

In 1971, Motorola, Incorporated, a diversified Chicago-based electronics corporation, sent a group of representatives to the Industrial Skill Center to determine if Motorola could expand on the

Center's operation by adding a further dimension to the industrial training the students were receiving.

The contingent gave an enthusiastic report, and Motorola's Automotive Products Division agreed to sponsor a testing and repair shop on the Center's first floor. Six thousand dollars was allotted for preparation of the work area, and equipment valued in excess of $50,000 was installed. Dick Palazzo, an engineering technician from the division's Franklin Park, Illinois, plant, volunteered to act as instructor and superintendent of the shop, with Motorola paying his salary. Operation began in November of 1971.

When a student attending high school on the second floor decides he would like to participate in the Motorola program, Palazzo admits him on a trial basis for one week. During that week, the student has the opportunity to become familiar with the operation and to learn, at the same time, what will be expected of him in the Motorola shop. Palazzo may observe the student to determine his willingness to contribute his own efforts toward completion of the training period.

The student receives no pay during the trial week and is given a list of electronics terms, with definitions, which he is asked to study. Toward the end of the week, he is given a test on the words, the results of which enable Palazzo to accurately judge the amount of work which the student is willing to do. If he passes the test, he is admitted to the program.

In the Motorola shop, the products of Motorola's Automotive Products Division are tested for possible defects and repaired, if necessary. This includes the complete line of automobile radios, tape players, voltage regulators, alternators, ignition systems and meters.

Lynn Lodge is a graduate of the Industrial Skill Center and the Motorola shop. He began work at Motorola's Franklin Park plant after leaving the Center. Within his first month of employment he reached 100 per cent productivity, which takes the average trainee about six months—a tribute both to the occupational education program and to Lodge himself.

Palazzo notes that there is no obligation for the students to look to Motorola for employment upon graduation, but they generally feel that since there is already a familiarity with the products, work required, norms, and expectations, that it is a natural step to apply for work with Motorola or a similar electronics company.

RULES

It is Philip Viso's belief that the structure of rules under which most high schools operate indicates that the school is somewhat inflexible to individual problems. Implied or explicitly stated in the rules is a concomitant punishment. Viso sees this as being counter-productive to a professed aim of school systems—that of giving students the responsibility to rely on their own self-control in pursuit of their education. It is for this reason that he instituted only one rule when he began the Center. This rule states only that the students must treat each other with mutual respect.

About the effectiveness of the rule, Viso says, "In the five-year history of the Center, it has not been necessary to change the rule or to add any more."

At the Industrial Skill Center, there is an effort to develop the student's own interest in attending without outside pressure being brought to bear. There is no attendance rule, yet attendance runs at 92.8 per cent.

The tardiness factor in the Center's shops is less than 3 per cent, and the walls are totally free of vandalism. The building's thousands of windows are all intact, a tribute to the respect of the students and the community toward the Industrial Skill Center.

RESULTS

In August of 1973, a group of 58 students graduated from the Center. Of this class, about 50 per cent continued their training in some type of advanced education. Twenty-five per cent of the class moved directly into jobs that they had lined up while in the school, and the remaining 25 per cent returned to traditional high schools to continue their education.

It is important to note here that none of the graduates left the Center without a plan for the future. The vast majority of the students, when they entered the Center, had been drop-outs from school. They had wandered from job to job, frequently with long periods of unemployment between jobs. Now, every graduate of the Center has a well-planned road to a successful future.

CASES

Rickey Frazier is a product of Chicago's South Side. He attended a Chicago high school until the age of 16. After leaving school, he says, "I roamed the streets and hung around the corner. I was like most of the guys in my community—no place to go but down. Nothing to look forward to but another day of frustration."

Frazier's cousin told him about the Industrial Skill Center. "When you're doing nothing, what can you lose?" said Frazier. After en-rolling, he studied in the Motorola shop under the direction of

Palazzo, in addition to taking academic courses. "I intended to make something out of myself, and I really worked at it," explained Frazier. "I took courses in English, science, history, and math and I majored in radio repair."

After studying for 18 months at the Center, he earned his high school diploma and was hired by Motorola as a radio repairman. In addition to this job, he now works as a part-time instructor at the Center.

McArthur Diggs says he was pushed out of his Chicago high school because of his gang activities. He was unemployed when he began to study at the Industrial Skill Center. There he earned his high school diploma, an Illinois State University scholarship and an Educational Opportunity Grant. He now studies pathology at a veteran's hospital and follows the pre-med curriculum in a dual enrollment program at Malcolm X College and the Chicago Circle Campus of the University of Illinois. Upon receipt of his physician's license, he plans to establish a medical practice in, what he calls, "the medical wasteland of Chicago's West Side."

Lynn Lodge moved to Chicago from Georgia, where he had completed his first two years of high school. In Chicago, he says he didn't care for the quality of the traditional high school, so he applied for admission to the Industrial Skill Center. He put his name on the school's waiting list and, after two months, was admitted.

The Industrial Skill Center enabled him to complete his remaining high school requirements in one year. He is now working for Motorola and is taking courses toward his degree in electrical engineering. About his education at the Center he says, "I had to work pretty hard, especially in the Motorola shop, but it sure has been worth it. I have a head start over most 17-year-old guys by having finished high school already.

"Mr. Viso gives the students the feeling that he really cares about them," said Lodge. "That's probably the reason why guys are finishing high school at the Center when they couldn't make it in other high schools. People everywhere have to know that there is someone who cares about whether they make it or not. Mr. Viso is always available to talk about problems; the whole staff is that way. They have gone down in the middle of the night to get guys out of jail."

About the packaged instructional materials, Lodge says, "It is an extremely effective method. I think other schools should start this program. Some of the students have problems with the material, but the teachers and even the other students try to help whenever they can. That's the whole idea of the Center—helping people.

"I've recommended the Center to some of my friends," he added. "It seems that if you're interested in finishing high school, but don't like regular classroom situations, you have to be interested in the Industrial Skill Center."

IN THE FUTURE

In May of 1973, Motorola was instrumental in drawing the interest of the Electronics Industries Association in participating in the Industrial Skill Center. Representatives of the EIA toured the Center and were impressed with this new educational concept.

An industry-wide contribution to the Center is scheduled to begin in early 1974. A shop will be established on the first floor of the building for the training of students in the repair of color television sets. Several major electronics manufacturers will provide funding for the program through the Association, and an instructor from the Center will be designated as the teacher/superintendent of the new shop.

Another result of Motorola participation in the Center has been that the National Alliance of Businessmen has become actively involved in promoting the Industrial Skill Center and in encouraging more industrial participation.

John Maloney is Motorola's manager of employee communications. He is on loan from Motorola to the NAB, where he is manager of all youth-oriented activities of the Alliance. He has arranged for a number of companies to tour the Skill Center to obtain a first-hand view of the operation and to see if they can participate.

Another project currently being considered by the staff of the Industrial Skill Center is a construction trades training program. This program would, as do the existing programs, revolve around actual work being done to produce a marketable end result.

As it has been proposed, the students in the construction trades program will have a series of classroom sessions on building skills. Later, a work crew consisting of students will completely renovate an area building. Federal funding for the project is currently being sought.

Also in future plans is an agreement with a major oil company to train automobile mechanics. The participating company will again provide expertise and equipment, and actual work will be done on automobiles in need of repair.

CONCLUSION

U.S. Congresswoman Cardis Collins, Illinois Seventh District representative, spoke at the August, 1973, graduation ceremony at the Center. Her remarks were basically along three lines:

1. She expressed her pleasure in the fact that industry has begun to participate in educational programs aimed at breaking the poverty cycle.

2. She stated that she is glad to see that so many young people, who would otherwise be roaming the streets, now have promising futures.
3. She noted that it is very gratifying to observe the cooperation between education and industry for the betterment of society.

In July of 1972, U.S. Senator Charles Percy of Illinois visited the Industrial Skill Center. He was given a tour of the building and talked extensively with students and faculty. On October 14, he gave a speech before the U.S. Senate in which he said:

The essence of the Skill Center idea is that high school students can be productive members of the work force and get paid for it while they pursue their high school education. In this new concept of high school education, half of the student's eight-hour day is devoted to academic endeavors and the remainder to industrial skills training through production of a marketable product. . . .

I am glad to see that someone has finally discovered a workable formula for blending public education with the private sector. I feel strongly that broader application of the Industrial Skill Center concept could have nation-wide ramifications by serving to more fully utilize America's human resources and revolutionize segments of our educational system.

It should be noted that Motorola's participation in the Industrial Skill Center is not entirely from purely altruistic motives. There is a definite benefit to the company as the result of basically two points:

1. The students at the Center, while they are learning about electronics in the Motorola shop, are providing a service to the company by analyzing and repairing radio parts, as part of the Automotive Products Division's quality assurance program.
2. The students, upon graduation, provide an ideal source of trained labor for the electronics industry. They have a solid background in electronics and are familiar with the industry.

Whether the company or the school receives greater benefits from this cooperation is academic; more importantly, this venture is showing that both industry and education can benefit from endeavors such as this.

Ray Orth is corporate director of employee services for Motorola. He has been instrumental in establishing the Motorola shop at the Center, and continues to be deeply involved with the operational aspects of the program. "It is a very satisfying experience when everyone involved can benefit from any venture. With the Skill Center, the school benefits, the company benefits, the student benefits and society, in general, benefits."

On a personal note, I would like to add that I am proud that Motorola is a part of the Industrial Skill Center. I believe that the concept of the Center will prove to be prolific, and it will make welcome changes in many segments of our society.

CHARLES J. PILLIOD, JR.

Charles J. Pilliod, Jr., was elected Chairman of the Board of The Goodyear Tire & Rubber Company on April 1, 1974.

He had been President of the company since July 19, 1972, and Chief Executive Officer since Jan. 1, 1974.

Pilliod previously had served as President of Goodyear International Corporation, a subsidiary, and as an Executive Vice President of the parent company.

The fourth man to serve as Chairman of the Board of the world's largest tire and rubber company, Pilliod joined Goodyear in 1941 as a production trainee.

He was born October 20, 1918, in Cuyahoga Falls, Ohio, a community almost within the shadow of Goodyear corporate headquarters in East Akron. He attended Muskingum College, New Concord, Ohio, and Kent State University, Kent, Ohio.

Pilliod was an Air Force pilot in World War II and rejoined Goodyear in 1945 as a sales staffman in the company's foreign operations.

He was appointed Managing Director of Goodyear-Panama in 1947 and four years later was transferred to the company's Peruvian subsidiary as an industrial rubber products representative.

In 1953, he was promoted to Assistant Sales Manager in Peru.

Successive moves found Pilliod serving as Sales Manager of Goodyear-Colombia in 1954 and as Commercial Manager of Goodyear-Brazil in 1956. He became Managing Director in Brazil in 1959.

In 1963, Pilliod was assigned to Goodyear-Great Britain as Sales Director. He became Managing Director there a year later.

Pilliod returned to Akron in 1966 as Director of Operations for Goodyear International, becoming a Vice President of the company a year later.

In January, 1971, he was elected President of Goodyear International and a Vice President of Goodyear Tire. His election as an Executive Vice President and a director of the parent company came in September, 1971.

Pilliod is a director of CPC International, Inc., the International Road Federation, the International Economic Policy Association, the American Graduate School of International Management, the Highway Users Federation for Safety and Mobility, the Rubber Manufacturers Association, the National Association of Manufacturers, and The Goodyear Bank.

He is a trustee of the Committee for Economic Development, the National Urban League, the United States Council of the International Chamber of Commerce, Akron Community Trusts, and Akron City Hospital.

Pilliod is a member of the Policy Advisory Committee for Trade Negotiations, Washington, D. C., the Tire Industry Safety Council, the Society of Automotive Engineers, the Ohio Transportation Research Center Advisory Council, and the Akron Area Council, Boy Scouts of America.

He also is a member of the Portage Country Club, Akron, the Sharon Golf Club, Sharon Center, Ohio, and the Laurel Valley Golf Club, Ligonier, Pa.

In March, 1972, the award of Honorary Commander of the Most Excellent Order of the British Empire (CBE) was conferred on Pilliod by Queen Elizabeth of Great Britain.

The CBE, highest recognition generally given by the British Empire to non-Britons, was awarded to Pilliod for "outstanding services in the cause of Anglo-American relations."

Pilliod and his wife, Marie Elizabeth, have three sons, Charles J., III, Mark Alan, and Stephen Matthew, and two daughters, Christine Marie and Renee Elizabeth.

Chapter 5

Used for a Purpose

CHARLES J. PILLIOD, JR.

A corporation's social responsibility is usually as wide or narrow as the minds of the men who have shaped or are shaping its policies and corporate tone or character.

Because those in top or middle management who shape the corporate ethos ultimately retire or leave a company for a variety of reasons, this sense of social responsibility changes, often subtly, through the years.

Then, too, community and national problems change in character and scope, requiring new approaches and new decisions.

Therefore there are no ironclad rules or permanent guidelines to govern what corporations should or shouldn't do year in and year out. Often we just do what we think is right and hope that time will prove us right.

I may be charged with being myopic, but I strongly feel that a corporation should put first things first, and that a corporation's first social responsibility is to remain financially healthy. Put another way, employees who have invested their talents and a good share of their lives, shareholders who have invested their money, and consumers who spend their money on our products are a corporation's primary social responsibility.

For "social responsibility" means that you are answerable to people, and in the case of a corporation this means concern for those whose lives you touch.

After *this* obligation is met, *then* the concerns of the community and the world beyond should be tackled with dispatch and with the degree of magnanimity that the company's resources can afford.

There is a definite correlation between the economic vitality of a company and just what it can do in the field of social responsibility. I, for one, foresee a growth of social consciousness in future years, but profits will have to keep pace with this new mood.

In short, it does you no good to be closely tuned-in to social responsibility if you do not have the wherewithal to tackle problem areas.

I am at odds with the view that corporations exist in a social vacuum, or as Emil Capouya of *The Nation* put it:

The corporation is almost completely invulnerable to attempts from within to turn its activities in the direction of fulfilling human needs. Besides the fact that its personnel have been trained to ignore these needs, the corporation has very special sanctions determining its conduct, and these reside in the profit and loss account.

Now I don't argue with the idea that a corporation has to make a profit to stay in business, but the statement that its personnel have been trained to ignore human needs is way off target, at least from what I have observed during my career. While corporations are not charitable institutions that can pass out money indiscriminately, neither are they penny-pinching Scrooges. The implication that they "brainwash" their employees not to care about others is, to say the least, ludicrous.

In this regard, I like what B. R. Dorsey, president of Gulf Oil Corporation, said at a management conference at the University of Texas: "Social responsibility of business need not mean a reduction of profits . . . and profits need not mean the reduction of social responsibility."

But corporations are not endowed foundations. We cannot afford the freewheeling luxury of constantly asking ourselves: "What cause shall we back today?"

Rather we have a continuing obligation to our workers and shareholders to stay in business and show a profit. Otherwise we go under and drag thousands with us.

Let me be specific. I believe we have a stronger obligation to a retired schoolteacher who has invested her savings in my company than we do to fund researchers trying to find the cause of the common cold.

Naturally we would like to do both. But given the choice of bankrolling the researchers or paying a fair dividend to the schoolteacher, I must in good conscience opt for the schoolteacher. Otherwise, we have broken a trust.

Don't mistake this for a satisfied "fat cat" philosophy. It's just that a corporation can't be all things to all men.

What we do to alleviate the ills of society *must* be done in context of what the corporation does on a day-to-day basis. In short, a corporation's leaders might be likened to the head of a household. Our immediate family comes first. That's where we spend most of our time and money. After that we can worry about distant relatives and neighbors and the people across town.

Okay. I've made the point that philanthropy starts with your own family. So now I return to what I said at the beginning: corporate social responsibility is usually as wide or narrow as the minds of the men who have shaped or are shaping the policies and corporate character.

At Goodyear, we have inherited a legacy for compassion. It began a long time ago.

Paul W. Litchfield, the man who forged Goodyear into the world's largest rubber company, was quick to recognize the importance of this trait.

He once wrote: "Some men have failed because they lived to themselves, shut humanity out of their thinking. Other men have succeeded because their love of humanity was so outstanding that doors flew open at their approach, and they got help and cooperation everywhere."

Litchfield went on, "It might not be out of place for me to cite one man in this connection—Charles W. Seiberling, one of the founders of Goodyear. People did not call him one of the great businessmen of his generation. They said his heart ran away with his head. But it was this very warmth and kindliness and good will which more than any other single factor built Goodyear in its formative years, created the teamwork, the family spirit, the fierce loyalty, and the response to emergencies, which had so much to do with bringing the company, in a dozen years, from one of the smallest in the field to leadership."

Since the time of such men as Litchfield and Seiberling, the codes of corporate management have been under assault in such books as *Up the Organization,*[1] *The Peter Principle,*[2] and *The Greening of America.*[3] Many of the ideas these books present seem on the surface quite convincing, yet when analyzed in the harsh light of reality, they often are guilty of being too simplistic, too utopian. Yet the new literature touches on a point that I fully agree with—that is, management has an obligation, wherever possible, to see that employees achieve a greater sense of personal satisfaction from what they do.

Along this line, Goodyear's early management strongly believed that there is a direct correlation between a healthy body and a man's ability not only to do his job well, but also to fully enjoy his hours away from work.

Thus, more than a half century ago a large gymnasium was built across the street from corporate headquarters in Akron, and it has been in constant use since.

We actively promote the idea of employees taking part in sports, and our company has leagues for basketball, flag football, softball, bowling, volleyball, and golf. And in the last few years membership in our skiing and racquet clubs has mushroomed.

Realizing that not everyone is cut out for active participation in sports, our company's 40 employees' clubs offer a varied menu of

[1]Townsend, Robert C.: *Up the Organization.* New York, Knopf, 1970.
[2]Peter, Lawrence J., and Raymond Hull: *The Peter Principle.* New York, Morrow, 1969.
[3]Reich, Charles A.: *The Greening of America.* New York, Random House, 1970.

interests, ranging from chess and bridge to gourmet eating and model railroading. Our 1,400-seat theater provides a fine setting for the Goodyear Musical Theater. And in recent years we have turned our 67-acre Wingfoot Lake Park into one of the finest employee facilities in the country.

All this costs money, but we consider it money well spent, because it shows our employees that we care about them over and beyond what they produce in the way of work.

The treating of employees as individuals and recognizing their private worth was closely examined by a Xerox executive, Roger D'Aprix, in his book *Struggle for Identity: The Silent Revolution Against Corporate Conformity.*[4] Despite its formidable title, the book scores a lot of telling points. D'Aprix believes the stereotyped Organization Man is being replaced by executives who want a reasonable, free society inside a corporation, and a broadening of traditional goals so that the organization serves society as well as itself. He emphasizes something that those in my company take for granted — that people should not be dealt with as inventory that depreciates, to ultimately be written off the books, but as autonomous human beings with psychic needs.

D'Aprix points out that "employees need to be recognized as members of a human community and as contributors to it. They need to be reasonably fulfilled in their work. They need to be dealt with as intelligent and mature beings who can be trusted to contribute to goals they understand."

At this juncture I would like to be slightly chauvinistic about my company in respect to another point that D'Aprix makes. He said that one problem with our affluent society is that many products and services are not useful in any concrete sense, so there is disquiet among employees because they feel that what they produce doesn't have any real value.

Happily, the company I've spent my adult years with doesn't fall into this category. In the three decades I've been with Goodyear, I have yet to see a frivolous geegaw manufactured. Because everything we make or design is utilitarian — tires, aircraft wheels and brakes, meat packaging material, inflatable greenhouses, rubber railroad crossings, automotive parts, and so on — our employees can go home at night feeling they have contributed to something useful.

Business has a social responsibility to communicate its ideas, policies and philosophy beyond its walls. We have an obligation to break down the barriers between us and the uninformed sector of the public and acquaint them with the new breed of industrial executives who have a vital concern for and the determination to shape a better society.

---

[4]D'Aprix, Roger M.: *Struggle for Identity: The Silent Revolution Against Corporate Conformity.* Homewood, Ill., Dow Jones–Irwin, Inc., 1972.

Therefore I disagree with such thinking as that of Professor Milton Friedman, an economist, who feels that the business of business is only business. He takes the position that the involvement of a corporation in acts of social responsibility is a dereliction by management of its obligation to shareholders. This attitude, that business has but one purpose, to enrich itself, and that nothing else matters, is just the type of thinking that has turned young people away from business as a career, and has provoked general cynicism.

Rather, I think, we now have a new generation of corporate leaders who are willing to accommodate the corporation to meet the new responsibilities in the changing economic and social climate of today.

Historically, though, as I said in the start, Goodyear has taken the position that its first responsibility is to its employees, shareholders, and consumers. It has been our corporate philosophy to encourage employees to actively take part in all areas of community involvement, ranging from politics and government to civic, fraternal, religious, and charitable organizations. In short, we want our people to pull their oar in the communities in which they live.

This involvement should not be restricted to the comfortable suburbs, but must extend to the inner cities, from which we get many of our employees. We must make this commitment if for no other reason than that our tax dollars and salaries provide much of the support of the cities.

We should heed the advice of John Gardner, head of Common Cause, who said:

In any city a high proportion of executive talent, analytical skill, and institutional strength lies outside city government. Unless these private sector strengths can be mobilized in behalf of public purposes, the community will not solve its problems.

Thus, it is incumbent upon business that it urge its members to assume roles of leadership in their communities if we are to build a better place in which to live and bring up our children.

But it's not enough to promote activism on the part of your employees. Like most corporations, Goodyear realistically and frankly recognized some years ago that it had not done all it could in the area of opportunities for minority people.

We set about changing that, and our attitude is reflected in this statement our chairman, Russell DeYoung, made to a group of company managers several years ago:

We are committed to programs of providing equal opportunity, regardless of race, creed, national origin or sex. The job of the equal opportunity department is to coordinate these programs throughout the company. These programs are a part of our life. We *must* lead our industry in providing equal opportunity in employment.

Today, I'm happy to say, the phrase "Equal Employment Opportunity Employer" is not a hollow catchword in my company, but is backed by concrete, progressive actions.

We have on our staff, reporting directly to top management, a manager of Equal Employment Opportunity and a coordinator of minority group development in the sales organization. They have the full support of our top management in their undertakings. We are happy with the strides that have been made, and with the receptive attitudes throughout the company.

As a consequence, more qualified black men and women than ever have moved into all phases of production, research, engineering and other key staff-line positions.

There's another area dealing with minorities of which Goodyear can be justifiably proud. That's our new dealer franchise program, in which we have been successful in encouraging minority individuals to go into business for themselves. In this program our company provides financial backing over and above the minimal investment that the individual is required to make, plus providing sales and marketing assistance.

We are doing something about training and aid to education for disadvantaged and minority groups. In our "Springboard" program, we provide work for young "hard-core" unemployed men during the summer at our Wingfoot Lake employees park. By this we hope to provide job readiness training to prepare these men for employment, whether it be for Goodyear or for another company.

We also take young women from the inner city schools and provide them with on-the-job training as typists. So far all have been hired for permanent positions after graduation.

Realizing that Negro colleges have a great need for financial assistance, we have a regular program of scholarship aid, and we have made grants and donations to the schools.

We have an aggressive program geared to recruit black college graduates. Because of the nature of our company, we often hire more engineers than any other kind of graduates, and there is tremendous competition for black engineers. These graduates, our recruiters tell me, are quick to ask questions about our company's position on social matters and community involvement. In looking over what other corporations have done or are doing, I don't think Goodyear has to take a back seat on this to anyone. And because we have a definitive policy on this, I foresee greater growth in this area of human relationships.

Sometimes business is mistaken for what it is not. Business is basically a doer; in the act more often than in the word its true nature becomes apparent. By its very attitude to those who have a claim on it — employees and their families, the stockholders who own the company, and the community in which it resides — business makes apparent not only its social role, but also its entire integrated part in society today.

An example of this is the way we use our three blimps in this country and another in Europe to better community communications. Seventy-five per cent of the messages carried by our blimps' colorful night signs are devoted to public service activities, urging people to take part in such worthy causes as the United Fund, Red Cross blood drives, and highway safety campaigns.

From what I've heard and observed, these hovering billboards in the sky carry a visual impact that can be achieved no other way. But urging people to become involved isn't the only social function our blimps serve. At different times they are used to help government agencies in research programs. State and local officials often use them as aerial platforms to study traffic snarls, to sample polluted air, and to try to find answers to various other ills that plague heavily populated areas. And the National Aeronautics and Space Administration has made use of them to study the problem of sonic booms. So these aerial ambassadors do much more than carry stark commercial messages. They contribute to meaningful projects.

The concern about others that marked the lives of our company's early leaders still thrives at Goodyear. We are still concerned about matters of the heart—literally. For more than a decade our researchers have been designing and building artificial hearts which some day may be implanted in man. This work, carried on without government subsidy, looks promising. Various configurations and materials have been used. One prototype kept an animal alive for 17 days. These hearts are sent out to private and public clinics without cost for study and evaluation. We know that our artificial hearts may never be used in sustaining human life, yet we are convinced that our particular expertise is advancing the state of the art.

For these contributions we expect neither credit nor a profit. We are, as our chairman, Russell DeYoung, said in discussing the social responsibility of business, "contributing to progress and the making of a better world."

In many of its undertakings to make this a better world, Goodyear has developed a policy of initiating projects, providing "seed money," and then letting communities bring them to fruition.

This is the role we have played in building artificial reefs that use discarded tires. The ability of tires to resist destruction has long been a bugaboo in community environmental efforts. Tires are not biodegradable; they continue to exist unchanged under all sorts of conditions.

Now, however, this very indestructibility of tires has proved to be an asset, and cast-off casings are providing a vital link in the environmental chain of life. They are being compacted, bound, and dropped to the ocean floor to provide a haven for fish and a spawning ground for many types of undersea life. Already fishermen along the East and Gulf coasts and in Australia are beginning to reel in fine catches over artificial reefs built of old tires.

In Fort Lauderdale, Fla., the project of building a reef of tires was tackled with community-wide enthusiasm under the auspices of a non-profit association. For this project, Goodyear has contributed a custom-built tire compacter, technical assistance, scrap tires, and "seed money."

On Florida's west coast, Goodyear is assisting a developer of a planned community on Marco Island in building a mile-long, half-mile-wide rubber reef that has attracted at least 33 species of fish, including some trophy-size catches. Here again we provided tires, compacting equipment and technical assistance. And in recent weeks, Goodyear has announced its association with two new reef projects at Naples and Ft. Myers, Fla.

Current estimates hold that annually nearly a million tires will go into the building of artificial reefs.

We have tackled this problem of old tires from many different angles, knowing we have an obligation to use them constructively.

One promising method is using them as fuel.

Nearing completion, Goodyear's new $550,000 boiler furnace at our Jackson, Mich., tire plant is designed to consume 3,000 scrap tires a day—more than a million a year. The smokeless, odorless furnace will process steam for the manufacture of new tires and, at the same time, meet rigid state and local air pollution standards.

I should point out that this unique furnace is *not* a money-saver for Goodyear. The cost of installation was considerably more than for a standard gas- or oil-fired boiler, and it will cost more to operate.

But our engineers are optimistic that further research will reveal ways to make this first-in-America furnace an all-important and economical link in the tire recycling and energy-saving chain.

Another approach we are trying is putting worn tires to use in highway safety. Laced together with cables, tires are being tested as crash barriers to protect motorists from fixed hazards, such as bridge piers at highway interchanges. Tests conducted at the University of Cincinnati and by the Texas Transportation Institute at Texas A & M University have proved they could reduce deaths and injuries at these hazardous points. Test cars hurtling at speeds of nearly 60 miles per hour have smashed into the cushioning devices head-on and have been absorbed much like a finger being jabbed into a stale marshmallow.

The testing has shown that, properly constructed, the tire barriers are capable of trapping a crashing car and absorbing the energy. One barrier has survived 17 test crashes without having to be replaced.

Not all of our efforts to put tires to work have proved economically successful. Our attempt to use chopped-up tire fragments held together with a rubber-based binder produced some beautiful-appearing artificial turf—but the installation cost, all done by hand, made it prohibitive, for us or for anyone else.

But our researchers are still hard at work trying to devise new methods for converting old tires to practical uses. Right now we're working on floating breakwaters, marker buoys, floating pipeline collars and ship bumpers.

Some may prove feasible and some may not. But, at least to my thinking, the important thing is we're trying to lengthen the list of recycling applications to improve our environment.

My company's anti-pollution efforts are not an on-again, off-again proposition. The cornerstone of our environmental control policy is embraced in a formalized statement to which we adhere:

Goodyear is committed to devote whatever time, scientific talent, engineering skills and funds that are necessary to establish the highest standards of environmental control in all our facilities and to foster such standards in the communities in which we live and work.

To assure conformity at all levels, we have a committee on environment—made up of representatives of the engineering, development, research, law, corporate planning, and public relations departments—that meets regularly to review problem areas, establish priorities, and see that plans and policies are carried out.

Moreover, Goodyear centralizes the responsibility for these functions in a manager of environmental engineering who has been given the clout to carry out these directives. He coordinates the activities of environmental specialists in our plants, for every domestic Goodyear plant employs an environmental engineering representative who coordinates local planning and submits periodic reports on plant pollution controls.

Our larger plants have full-time managers of environmental engineering who report directly to a three-member corporate staff. Our smaller plants delegate environmental protection responsibilities to specialists who also report to the corporate staff.

No purpose would be served citing in detail the millions of dollars Goodyear has spent or committed to protect our environment or enumerating individual accomplishments.

Rather, it is my conviction that a company's awareness of problems and its willingness to correct them, or better yet, to avoid creating them in the first place are what determine if it is a good corporate citizen.

Goodyear is no newcomer to the realm of conservation and ecological concern. Our company began sponsoring a nationwide conservation program (The Goodyear Conservation Awards Program) a quarter of a century ago—long before attention was focused on the problems of effective resource management.

Since this program started, it has encouraged hundreds of soil and water conservation districts, and their cooperating landowners and users, in their battle to conserve America's resources.

Our environmental efforts have not gone unnoticed. As this is being written, Goodyear was notified that it had won the top national award for environmental protection by Keep America Beautiful, Inc., a non-profit service organization.

None of this would have been possible if the company did not make a profit. Profit constitutes the wages of capital—and without profit payrolls cannot be met nor can a corporation's social responsibility be fulfilled. Along these lines, I like what Judson Bemis, president of Bemis Company, Inc., had to say in discussing business responsibilities to society.

In order to be profitable over the long term, a company can only operate in the public interest. The public interest may change with changing conditions over the years, but the basic fact is that a company cannot succeed over the long term unless it has the confidence of the public.

This, I believe, is a true assessment of the public's attitude, and is the main reason our company has become the leader in the rubber industry.

Goodyear also believes that a part of its social responsibility is to perpetuate the free enterprise system that has brought about the high standard of living America enjoys. It's foolhardy—for those of us who believe in the competitive system—to stand mutely at the sidelines and let critics pelt us. We believe we have an obligation to tell the business story to the government, to labor, to educators, and to the public before controls weaken us to the point of anemia. We are working on a number of approaches, including programs directed toward young people.

Like many corporations, we are concerned about some of the opinions being passed to the young by some instructors in the very colleges we support with contributions and scholarships. So, after reviewing our support, we decided that we couldn't be faulted for not wanting to feed the hand that bites back at the free enterprise system. As a result of this study, Goodyear is now making a $250,000 grant each to the University of Akron and Kent State University Colleges of Business Administration for Endowed Chairs in Free Enterprise. The objective is to promulgate the free enterprise system and encourage the entrepreneurial spirit. The grants are for an initial five-year period, and are subject to periodic review by the two universities to insure the program is meeting its stated objectives. Goodyear doesn't ask for the privilege of review for itself, because it doesn't want to be accused of interfering with academic freedom. But we are confident that the universities will adhere to the spirit and intent of the program.

Eventually we may broaden the program to still other colleges, perhaps using such chairs to replace some of the support we've been giving to such institutions in other ways. For Goodyear feels that unshackled private enterprise must be promoted on a positive key, and not always be put in a position of defending itself from detractors whose motives often stem from self-aggrandizement.

Goodyear believes it is right to do battle to preserve this system of free enterprise, and not stand idly by while it is under attack. And that is why we are a major sponsor of the Junior Achievement Program, the "learn-by-doing" free enterprise program for youngsters in high school. It is also why W. R. (Dick) Bryan, our executive director of community services, makes numerous speaking appearances annually to speak out on the vital subject.

I am reminded of what Theodore Roosevelt, who personified many fine human traits, said: "Aggressive fighting for the right is the noblest sport the world affords." And the battle for the minds of the young is perhaps the most important battle of all. We must give young people an accurate concept of the free enterprise system so that they can judge it fairly and accurately. With this in mind, we are working toward this objective with youth *below* college level.

To help the high schools in Akron do a better job of explaining business to their students, we engaged one of our retired executives to draw up material for a pilot course on the business system. The four-week course zeroed in on the American business system, what makes it tick, and the role that corporations play in it. It made the point that corporations are not sinister organizations that try to control society—that they are simply groups of people joined together for a common purpose: to do business. This course is being further evaluated by both the school system and Goodyear.

We must remember that our children, in just a few short years, will be shouldering all the responsibilities and problems that we are not handling or are mishandling. And that they will have challenges we can't even envision today. Consequently, I feel that it's never too early to give them an inkling of what free enterprise is all about. Or to tell them that they, like us, will have to fight to preserve it.

We should let them know early that it is going to be a tough fight all the way, because there are those who feel that the work ethic runs against the grain—that there is an easier, softer way to get through life.

I think that those who would dodge away from deep commitment and hard work are wrong. We can't sit back and reap the rewards of others' sweat. We must, I feel, get across that involvement and daily dedication pay off in deep satisfaction. I am reminded of the approach that George Bernard Shaw had toward life. This iconoclastic playwright, who championed so many causes that we accept as facts of life these days, wrote:

I want to be completely used up when I die. The harder I work, the more I live. This is the true joy in life—the being used for a purpose recognized by yourself as a mighty one—being thoroughly used up when you are thrown on the scrap heap.

This, I believe, is what life is all about. If, by power of example, we can impart this attitude to the young, we will have provided a great legacy for our children and the generations ahead.

Chapter 6   Learning by Doing

RICHARD L. KATTEL

WILLIAM JENNINGS
VANLANDINGHAM

Richard L. Kattel attended Valley Forge Military Academy, Emory University, and the Program for Management Development, Harvard Business School.

He joined Citizens and Southern National Bank as Management Trainee in operations in 1958. In 1968 he became Assistant Cashier, in 1962 Operations Officer, and in 1963 Assistant Vice President. Two years later he assumed the post of Executive Vice President of the C&S National Bank, Savannah, and in 1971 became Director and President of the bank. In 1974 he became its Chairman and President.

He is also Trustee and Chairman of Citizens and Southern Realty Investors, Director of Peachtree Equity Securities, Inc., and officer and director of various C&S subsidiaries. In addition, he is director of numerous outside organizations and was General Chairman of the 1974 United Way Campaign of Metropolitan Atlanta.

William J. VanLandingham is an Executive Vice President of the Citizens and Southern National Bank. He is responsible for managing the bank's Public Affairs Department and the C&S Community Development Corporation (CDC), a wholly owned subsidiary of the C&S National Bank. CDC is designed to respond to the needs of improved housing and increased ownership of housing and businesses by low-income Georgians. In this capacity, Mr. VanLandingham is responsible for the expenditure of over $1 million annually on community-related projects through a statewide system of banks.

Mr. VanLandingham is a graduate of Georgia Institute of Technology, has studied at the Emory University School of Law, and attended the Program for Management Development at the Graduate School of Business Administration, Harvard University.

Upon graduation from college, Mr. VanLandingham served a tour of duty as a naval officer. After being discharged from the Navy, he was employed as a Production Manager by The Procter and Gamble Company. He served in this capacity for three years, before accepting a position with Rich's, Inc., as Assistant to the Vice President. It was at Rich's, the south's largest retail department store and a front-runner in community citizenship, that Mr. VanLandingham first began to see the positive effects of corporate social responsibility.

In 1966, he joined the C&S National Bank, serving as Assistant Comptroller before being promoted to Assistant Vice President and Director of the state-wide Georgia Plan. The Plan, which became a landmark in the realm of corporate social responsibility, called for the reinvestment of bank profits in Georgia communities through efforts to clean up blighted city ghettos. Results of the Georgia Plan were a reclamation of rundown city housing, the establishment of over 150 new, well-equipped playgrounds in low-income areas, and traveling dental buses that supply free dental care to underprivileged children. The C&S Community Development Corporation evolved from these efforts and operates under Mr. VanLandingham's guidance. CDC makes home ownership for low-income citizens a reality by supplying down-payment money in the form of a second mortgage, so that a conventional mortgage can be obtained. In addition, CDC encourages minority entrepreneurship by providing equity capital and management assistance to those who show character and capability in their fields.

Mr. VanLandingham believes in active civic participation and holds offices in a number of organizations. Among others, he serves on the Boards of Directors of the Georgia Institute of Technology National Alumni Association; Research Atlanta, Inc.; the Public Affairs Council; the Georgia Safety Council; and the Metro Atlanta Chapter of the American National Red Cross. He is a member of the Public Affairs Research Council of The Conference Board, and the Executive Committee for Urban and Community Affairs of the American Bankers Association. Mr. VanLandingham was recently selected as the Metro Atlanta Chairman of the National Alliance of Businessmen. He was voted one of the five outstanding young men of Atlanta in 1972 and appeared in *Who's Who in America* and the Outstanding Young Men in America publications. He is married to the former Mary Dell Cawley of Walterboro, South Carolina, and has two children, William Jennings, II, and Terri Leigh.

Learning by Doing

RICHARD L. KATTEL and
WILLIAM J. VANLANDINGHAM

THE GEORGIA PLAN—1968–1974 AND BEYOND

In 1968, Savannah, Georgia, like other cities across the country, was painfully aware of the contrasts between progress and decay that existed within it. Federal poverty programs were active in the city, but had failed to provide anything more than a string of empty promises to the low-income (predominantly black) community. Savannah's slums were draining the human resources of disadvantaged citizens in this proud and historic city.

A group of black citizens who felt that the time had come for action got together to see what course they might pursue. They knew that Mills Lane, a Savannah native and at that time president of The Citizens and Southern National Bank, had vast resources through the C&S bank that might offer some help, so they came to him with their request. It was Mr. Lane's feeling that the most effective way to remedy problems *of the community* was *action by the community,* and he suggested that they work together to come up with a plan for revitalization of living conditions within Savannah. The plan they drew up came to be known as the "Savannah Plan." The first step was to be a master two-day clean-up of selected target areas of Savannah. We called that "Spring Cleaning." It took place on May 17 and 18, 1968.

For Spring Cleaning to be effective, it had to be a total community effort, so schools, colleges, city government, civic groups, churches, and, most importantly, the residents of the target clean-up areas were included early in the planning and implementation stages. The business community pledged trucks, wreckers, and equipment, and our bank provided incentives to the residents in the form of free fencing, garbage cans, and an American flag to those who did a good job.

79

For the citizens of that 109-block area of Savannah slums, Spring Cleaning was a complete success. Ten thousand volunteers from all over town removed 150 tons of debris and 78 junked autos, and the local residents had tasted a bit of an opportunity to improve their standard of living by their own efforts.

The Savannah Plan was conceived as a practical demonstration that any community can, on a do-it-yourself basis with no governmental assistance, revitalize its living and business environment. It was based on several fundamental assumptions. The first is that a democracy means doing the most for the most people. Second, we assume that everyone wants to improve his standard of living. Third, we assume that the incentive method is the best way to accomplish things. And fourth, we assume that, as a last resort, government will step in to fill needs when business does not.

What we were saying to the people of Savannah was that for this experiment, we would be the catalyst, providing resources, leadership if necessary, and organizational ability if required. In addition, we would provide moral support to help overcome the arbitrary obstacles which might be the products of prejudice or ignorance themselves.

We were not interested in a give-away. Nor were we interested in legislating or dictating the type of long range effects which might result from our efforts. For these, there were no long range schemes or grand designs.

The experiment was successful. We found that the participants not only were receptive to it, but took the ball and ran faster than we did. As a direct result of Spring Cleaning participation, schools, churches, civic groups, and businesses found needs within disadvantaged areas that they could fill. Churches started day care centers and interfaith chapels; colleges began tutorial projects; civic groups built playgrounds and community centers. Many businesses broadened their hiring practices, offering assistance and counseling to small businesses in ghetto areas, donating land for playgrounds, and sponsoring boys' clubs and scout troops.

The Savannah Plan, then, was the experience that brought people of different backgrounds together and gave them a common goal. It was the mechanism that opened communications channels closed since the Civil War. It caused people to ask questions and, perhaps, caused some people to finally reject the parameters of their existence which they had accepted as fact for so long. Many of the initial steps, including Spring Cleaning, which were used so successfully in Savannah to start the ball rolling were undertaken successfully again in 11 other Georgia cities, including Atlanta, and as these steps were taken, the Savannah Plan rapidly became the Georgia Plan.

Several months ago, two university professors doing a case study on the Spring Cleaning projects asked why we don't still continue to do these projects year after year. They were concerned that because we were not doing that same clean-up program each year, we were backing off from a commitment to do the kind of thing that program stood for. These gentlemen failed to understand a couple of characteristics of our style of doing business.

First, we understand that what works for today may not do for tomorrow, and to institutionalize a particular effort may be just the poison that kills it. We never intended for Spring Cleaning to be an end in itself. It was simply a vehicle that got those who needed help and those who wanted to help traveling in the same direction.

Second, we define "citizenship" as "the reinvestment of our leadership and corporate resources to improve the economic climate, from which we ultimately expect to derive a profit." The profit is a secondary goal which may not be realized for many years. Our immediate goal is improvement of the economic surroundings of those we are working with. Unless the citizens involved are going to benefit materially and economically, and be better able to make a living— thus both putting more into and taking more out of life—an assistance project should not be undertaken.

Over the past five years, many of the original priority needs have been met, and new priorities have developed. At the same time, our ability to respond to the priorities of the day has improved a great deal. We have gone a bit beyond Spring Cleaning, but the fundamental principles which inspired that program remain intact. We still don't want to be a part of any give-aways. Nor do we want to participate in a plan done primarily as a public relations effort. And finally, we still believe that private enterprise and the incentive system are better tools for the community to use in self-improvement than the government.

THE COMMUNITY DEVELOPMENT CORPORATION

The second major step in implementing the objectives of the new Georgia Plan followed almost immediately on the heels of Spring Cleaning. Seeing the results of their own efforts in improving their immediate physical environment, the citizens in these clean-up areas were motivated to seek further economic improvements—better housing, better jobs, ownership of homes and businesses. They needed support, however, in the form of financing in order to be able to carry out their desires. It was to provide this missing element that the Community Development Corporation (CDC) was formed.

The CDC was established as a separate corporation for several reasons. It gave some visible and tangible identity to the efforts of the bank and the community. As a separate corporation it could do some things which the bank could not legally do alone, such as making second mortgage loans, building houses for resale, experimenting with new housing ideas, owning, refurnishing and renewing real estate for sale. Also, the grouping of assets like these in one place had the additional benefit of isolating them from the criticism of the bank examiners.

The CDC was capitalized in 1968 with $1,000,000 taken directly from bank profits. Another million was added in 1970, and $1.5 million added in 1973. It now has offices in each of the 11 Georgia communities in which C&S has branches or subsidiary banks.

The objectives of the Corporation were two-fold: to seek solutions to the housing problems of low-income and minority citizens, and to provide ways of assisting these citizens in business undertakings.

In August, 1969, the CDC purchased Riverside Gardens Apartments in Savannah. The CDC paid a total of $154,254 and assumed a 4 per cent FHA mortgage for $105,730, which will be paid out in 1975. Over $320,000 has been spent by the CDC in renovating the 132-unit complex.

Originally built in 1942 to house wartime dock workers, the 22-acre project was owned by an out-of-state landlord who collected rents while the apartments deteriorated. Virtually no maintenance was done on the units during the 10 years prior to 1969, during which time the project became one of Savannah's worst low-income areas. Prostitution, drug abuse, and violent drunkenness were prevalent. Two murders were committed in the project a year before CDC purchased the development.

After purchase, the CDC completely renovated the apartments, inside and out. As one unit was stripped and renovated, another was kept available for the displaced family until work on their apartment was completed.

A laundromat and recreation hall, which also serves as a church, were built by the Corporation and a new playground was equipped. A kindergarten was organized by a local church, and a Boy Scout Troop was started.

All renovation work was handled by three minority contractors and financed through the CDC.

The results in terms of living improvement were heartening although the effort has been far from directly profitable. Rents have been raised somewhat since purchase, but are still low in comparison to the worth of the apartments. The current rent structure ranges from $51.50 for a one-bedroom apartment to $90.00 for a four-bedroom, two-bath unit. In recent years, the demand for the housing has declined with the construction of newer, federally funded housing projects nearby. But occupancy still remains above

80 per cent. Incidents of crime, which dropped dramatically when the project was renovated, have remained extremely low, and local educators indicate great improvement among the children who live there.

In that same year (1969) the Corporation purchased Tatnall Square, a city block of "slum property" located in a low-income, racially mixed Savannah neighborhood. On this block were three buildings which had been subdivided into apartments. Two of the buildings were reworked to offer more conveniently sized and vastly upgraded apartments, and the third was converted to a day-care center which is operated by a local non-profit organization. Renovation costs of these three buildings totaled over $209,000. All work was done by a local, CDC-financed contractor.

HOME OWNERSHIP PROGRAMS

While the work with the rental property met some obvious immediate needs and transformed slums into desirable areas, we were most interested in pursuing the activities which would lead to owner-occupied housing.

It was our observation that the lack of individual home ownership by citizens in disadvantaged areas is a major factor in the physical decaying of ghetto communities. Home ownership, we thought, would give the resident both an economic and social stake in his community, as well as provide an incentive to maintain and improve his surroundings. In researching the question, we found that approximately 95 per cent of Georgia's citizens in the lowest economic level did not own their own home. But significantly, we also found that the vast majority of this group had no trouble meeting their monthly rent payment.

What was needed was a way to transfer monthly rent payments into monthly mortgage payments.

THE MORTGAGE LOAN

A major obstacle for most families was meeting even the most liberal down payment requirements. At that time, federal subsidizing programs such as Operation Breakthrough and the 235 programs had not been developed. Therefore, the CDC developed a plan for providing down-payment money in the form of second mortgages through normal channels. These second mortgage loans are made at standard interest rates, but the terms are extended in order that the mortgage payments can fit into the budget of low-income families.

This is how the program works: Mortgage loan referrals to CDC are made through real estate agents or through the 110 C&S branches throughout Georgia. Incidentally, one of the reasons the program has been so effective, we feel, is that through our statewide network of banks, we have a front-row seat on housing communities throughout the state, are sensitive to the housing (and business) needs in their areas and are committed to seeing them met.

Applications are accepted from families who do not currently own property and whose income level is generally between $5,000 and $10,000 per year. With a few exceptions, the sales prices of the homes financed range between $8,000 and $20,000.

The CDC also accepts applications for loan assumptions if all other criteria are met. Applications for investment purchases (such as purchase-rent agreements) are not accepted.

After familiarization with the plan, an in-depth interview is conducted by the CDC loan officer, preferably with both husband and wife present. The real estate agent, if involved, may make the appointment, but preferably will not be present during the interview so as not to inhibit the applicants.

During the interview, a loan application is completed in detail. In addition to the basic information, the loan officer also obtains the following information:

1. Immediate supervisor's name.
2. Current landlord or resident manager's name.
3. Personal references other than job or family.
4. All past as well as current credit history.
5. Bankruptcy or wage earner history.
6. Past problems in criminal court.
7. Address and present owner's name for the house being purchased.

Next, the loan officer and applicant complete a budget worksheet together, listing the family's total net income and all expenses.

The approximate monthly mortgage payments are calculated and discussed with the family. The extra expense and "hidden costs" of purchasing a home are also explained, including the need and cost of an attorney's services, closing costs, utility connections, taxes and insurance, moving costs, maintenance expenses, and others. The loan officer also explains what his next step will be in processing the application, including credit reports, reference and employment checks, and so forth. This disclosure to the applicant is standard procedure, and it forms an open relationship for questions and discussions at the outset.

Before the applicant leaves the interviewer's office, he also receives two booklets to assist him in his new venture. The first, prepared by CDC, is "How to Take Care of Your Home" and discusses the responsibilities of the homeowner—taxes, insurance, utility agreements, maintenance. The second is on personal money management.

The loan officer then begins a complete investigation based on the application. Particular attention is given to past credit history, current financial situation, rental payment history, supervisory checks as to the applicant's work record, and reference checks.

If the loan application appears feasible, an appraisal is made on the house. The appraisal can be made either by a professional appraiser (paid for by the purchaser) or by a CDC loan officer capable of appraising the property (at no cost to the buyer). Deficiencies in the house are noted and explained to the agent or customer. In some instances a letter is sent to the current owner requiring that corrections be made before the loan can be closed. If more extensive repairs are indicated, the owner may be advised that CDC cannot finance the house in its present condition.

Up to 25 per cent of the total loan value of the property can be financed by a second mortgage. The CDC places the loan in its Mortgage Loan Portfolio and services all loans directly. Because of the inherent risk of the transactions and second mortgage position, the loans are amortized over a period of seven to 10 years at a rate of 6 per cent add-on—the same rate charged for most retail loans in the C&S Bank.

The first mortgage loan may be placed in a competitive bank or mortgage company, a savings and loan institution, the C&S Mortgage Company, or with the seller. The latter is sometimes an excellent first mortgage arrangement for the customer, since the seller may require only a nominal return as the mortgagee. Amortization will depend on the age and condition of the house as well as the current market schedule of the lender. The majority of first mortgage loans are amortized over 15 to 20 years in the C&S Mortgage Company, with loans placed in other institutions generally being amortized over 25 to 30 years. First mortgage loans are made at the prevailing conventional mortgage rate.

Escrow accounts for taxes and insurance are preferred on the first mortgage loans. At the beginning of the program, this was not done and often resulted in the need for follow-up action by CDC staff to effect proper insurance coverage.

In perfecting each second mortgage loan, a deed to secure debt, title search, appraisal, and insurance policy (payable to the CDC for the amount of the second mortgage) are retained in the customer's file along with the application information. The payment date is made flexible to fit the customer's monthly budget, and does not necessarily coincide with the first mortgage payment.

To date, approximately one in every two applications has been approved. When the application is denied, however, we have found that it is absolutely essential that the applicant understand why. If a current credit overload prevents approval of the loan, the applicant is advised to first discharge the obligation and apply again.

On the other side of the coin, we have found that the CDC loan officer must be fully aware of the problems encountered by low-income families. Considerable judgment and research are required, particularly where past credit problems are revealed. Such problems are more often the rule than the exception in low-income families, and the loan officer must determine whether they are a result of character or circumstance, then weigh the loan decision against the applicant's current financial status.

As with any lending situation, not all of the CDC housing loans have moved smoothly through payout. The majority of these past-due loans, however, are of the 15 to 29 day category and do not get any worse. In handling them, we send each past-due customer a personal letter asking for payment and offering counseling if financial problems are preventing payment from being made on time. Our experience has indicated we get a better response to a personal letter or phone call than to a form letter. These personal contacts stress the need to stay in touch with CDC when problems occur so that arrangements can be made to assist the customer. Also, coordination with the first mortgage holder is essential on past-due accounts, particularly if the first mortgage is held in another institution.

Our overall experience has been extremely gratifying. Through December 31, 1973, CDC investments of $1.25 million had enabled 378 families to own their own homes. Only six of these loans had gone sour, for total charge-offs of $8,284.

We believe four factors contributed to the program's success.

1. There must be an actual community need for such a program, which will guarantee sufficient volume.
2. The institution must be genuinely committed to make the program work and arrange adequate staffing and funding.
3. The initial analysis of each applicant's financial situation must be thoroughly and carefully done by a trained lending officer who is aware of low-income problems.
4. Follow-up on past due loans must be timely.

With these ingredients, the second mortgage program can be successful. Our experience has shown it to work.

EXPERIMENTS IN LOW-INCOME HOUSING

In addition to the financing need, the bank also found a lack of good quality low-income housing and has directed some of its efforts to this area.

In 1968, a city block was purchased by the CDC in Savannah as a site for new low-income housing at a purchase price of $50,000. The property was located in the downtown area of Savannah, surrounded by dilapidated rental units, but very accessible for shopping and transportation lines. The site was selected for these factors but also for another reason: to attempt to show that private enterprise could build low-income housing in an area previously considered "undesirable." Long range plans were to construct the housing, sell to low-income families and, in effect, begin to turn the neighborhood around. Profit would be minimized in order to sell the units at a reasonable price and apply the recouped cost in another housing project.

Labor leaders were contacted and it was agreed to reduce the ratio of foremen to journeymen in order to lower construction expense. The concept of private enterprise producing this type of housing at a reasonable cost was the key factor in accomplishing this cooperation.

In April, 1970, construction began on 30 condominium townhouses. Built to enclose a central courtyard, each townhouse featured two bedrooms, central heating and air conditioning, built-in kitchen, small private courtyards, individual outdoor gas grills, and ample storage. Each unit contains approximately 1,050 square feet of floor space. Total construction costs were approximately $425,000.

The project has been completed for two years, and, frankly, the location has been a deterrent in selling the units. We remain convinced, however, that basic improvements in a neighborhood have a ripple effect and serve to inspire the same types of improvement in surrounding areas. If we can instill this feeling into potential buyers who, by taking the initiative, not only would gain better housing themselves but would also serve as an example for others, we will still achieve our objectives. We think it's worth pursuing and have pledged ourselves to an aggressive educational campaign in this direction this year, with the goal of 100 per cent occupancy by year end.

Two experiments have actually been undertaken to examine new construction techniques and materials for low-cost housing. The first, in 1971, utilized reinforced concrete construction in which the houses, circular in form, were poured into removable fiberglass molds erected on concrete slabs. The plan included five rooms totaling almost 1000 square feet. The houses were of a type which had been built previously in Florida with some success.

Five of the units were constructed as an initial effort at a cost of $12,500 a piece, including $2,000 for the individual lots themselves. The finished units sold for $14,000 to $17,500, including land and all interior furnishings.

We discovered that the concrete construction in this design, although it was well suited for Florida, was not at all suited for the Atlanta climate. From the outset, tenants claimed that the homes were both difficult to cool and expensive to heat. Walls "sweated" and doors and windows didn't close or open well.

Repeatedly we attempted to work with the tenants to iron out their difficulties. Heating and cooling consultants made on-site inspections to determine what could be done to improve the situation, but they met with only limited success. In all but two instances, the houses were ultimately vacated and are now uninhabitable.

Out of the experience we also learned that these new homeowners knew very little about rudimentary home maintenance or repair, and they were unfamiliar with even a basic understanding of how to conserve energy in heating and cooling the homes. Several of them found the floor plan of the homes objectionable, but because of the construction techniques used, there was no possibility of economically remodeling them once the houses were completed. Two of the individuals "didn't like the neighborhood."

The project was ultimately abandoned by virtue of the combination of inappropriate construction techniques and a completely unprepared owner, but we learned from the experience, and we are trying again.

This time, we are using a design which features prefabricated aluminum construction and offers a variety of options to the potential owner, but the purpose of the project again is to see if housing of reasonably good quality can be built at a cost moderate enough for the low-income working person to afford.

The three-bedroom homes, including kitchen, utility shed, and carport, will total 1232 feet of living space and will sell for approximately $18,000 to $20,000. The plans, which have already received FHA approval, include new construction techniques and materials which have enabled us to cut building costs by 33 per cent. One demonstration home is being built, and additional homes will be constructed as requested. This time, the builder, the purchaser, and the lender will be able to work together to insure that the end result is a product that satisfies the expectations of us all.

BUSINESS OWNERSHIP PROGRAMS

Our business lending program was developed to provide the necessary equity capital without which low-income citizens had been unable to develop their own skills and resources and turn them into business opportunities. The criteria for CDC business loans place the emphasis on character and ability as well as collateral. A premium is also placed on hard work and the businessman's desire to meet his goals.

Through experience, we have developed credit criteria and evaluation methods specifically geared to this particular program. For analysis, the credit criteria of the CDC can be divided into three major categories.

1. Management Ability. In most circumstances there is no "track record" by which we can judge an applicant in the business loan program. Therefore, the alternative is to base our investigations on past work experience in the selected business—if the applicant has had any.

We also conduct extensive research into the applicant's character through means of employer, neighbor, and community references. In addition, a check is made into the applicant's personal credit history.

The upper and lower limits of credit acceptability are governed by the factors stated above. Specifics are best illustrated by examples.

UPPER LIMITS (loan decision "yes")

a. Approximately five years' experience as Assistant Manager of the same type of business.

b. Some management or supervisory responsibility within that type of business.

c. Very definite desire to own the type of business he has selected.

d. Applicant realizes that immediate personal profits may be depressed until the business gets on its feet.

e. Willingness to work full-time in the business.

LOWER LIMITS (loan decision "no")

a. No previous experience in the selected business or any managerial or supervisory positions.

b. Applicant worked in the related business previously, but quit because he did not like the work.

c. Does not have an intense desire to own his own business or has several "alternative" businesses he would like to attempt.

d. Personal income projections are unrealistic.

e. Applicant wants only a "part-time" business or to be an absentee manager.

f. An in-depth probing interview reveals apparent insufficient job or management knowledge.

2. Ability to Repay the Loan. Any commercial loan is made on the basis that it will be repaid from business-derived income. Each applicant is asked to calculate his income and expense projections, no matter how rudimentary; and the loan officer will assist, as needed. The repayment schedule is tailored to meet these projections.

An example of the upper and lower boundaries of the repayment ability decision would be as follows:

UPPER LIMITS (loan decision "yes")

a. Income projections are realistic and attainable.

b. Applicant realizes that his loan should be retired as quickly as his business will allow.

c. Applicant is fully aware that repayment will come from business profit.

LOWER LIMITS (loan decision "no")

a. Income projections are unrealistic or the applicant cannot be persuaded to be more conservative in regard to estimates of early performance.

b. Applicant requires a very extended repayment schedule or wishes to make only "token" repayments.

c. Loan repayment is to come from "outside" sources, in other words, his wife's income, part-time job, or other.

d. Windfall profit expectation.

3. The Business Must Provide Some Community Benefit. Businesses financed through CDC must generally accrue some benefit to the community as well as to the owner. For example, one-man operations are not generally considered as worthwhile as multi-job opportunities, since greater benefits can be gained from the businesses that hire. During the initial interview, "citizenship responsibility" is discussed with the applicant. This emphasis has resulted in such positive benefits to the community as job training, Little League sponsorship, and activity in volunteer organizations. Some examples of the type of businesses we might finance are manufacturing operations, contractors, quality retail outlets, industrial cleaning services, dry cleaners, restaurants, and printers. Not acceptable would be night clubs, pool halls, liquor stores, or social clubs.

The staff of the CDC is available to the businessman at all times. In addition, a C&S officer or management associate capable of rendering managerial assistance is often assigned to assist in any way possible. Just recently, we have also added to the CDC staff an accountant whose primary responsibility is to help these new businessmen with their management information problems. On several occasions, he has been able to work out some problem loans by dissecting the firm's accounting practices and showing the owner what he should do. As far as we know, there are few lenders who go this far in providing management assistance. Without access to such help, however, we feel the borrower will be at a disadvantage from the day he opens his doors for business. Money cannot be loaned and the borrower's other needs ignored; success depends equally upon capital and expertise, either inherent or acquired. The availability of such additional help is a vital part of the CDC program, allowing close scrutiny of the firm's progress or change in direction, if warranted, to insure success.

Loan rates in the CDC are the same as those offered in the C&S Bank. However, amortization and repayment plans can be extended to allow a reasonable repayment plan. When conditions beyond the borrower's control begin to affect his ability to repay, we may even arrange for extensions or reworking of the repayment schedule. For instance, we realize that economic downturns such as we experienced in 1973 often hit the small businessman the hardest, and we try in every way possible to help him weather the storms.

TABLE 6-1 PROFILE RESULTS*

Factors	Per Cent of Successes or Potential Successes		Per Cent of Charge Offs or Potential Losses	
	YES	No	YES	No
Managerial ability determined prior to loan	70	30	9	91
Sufficient character references	90	10	25	75
Highly competitive or risky business	80	20	75	25
Adequate records (bookkeeper or CPA)	100	0	29	71
Personal monetary investment	70	30	29	71
Initial income projections furnished	90	10	29	71
Managerial or supervisory experience	60	40	33	67
Loans and discussions documented	90	10	33	67
Equipment and inventory projections	90	10	33	67
Management Associate assigned to business	40	60	33	67
Realistic written goals established	90	10	37	63
Goals established after problems arose	–	–	42	58
Loan periodically reviewed by management	50	50	42	58
Customer lost interest in business	–	–	46	54
Customer had previous banking experience	100	0	62	38
Personal indebtedness excessive in beginning	20	80	33	67
Previous experience in selected business	60	40	33	67
Excessive personal withdrawals	10	90	33	67
"Fire engine" loans made	–	–	33	67
Relatives or friends employed	20	80	33	67
Business location good	80	20	71	29
Previous bankruptcy or wage-earner	0	100	29	71
Purchases made before discussion with CDC	20	80	25	75
Cooperative	100	0	79	21
Prior job stability good	100	0	88	12

*This is a tabulation of information compiled from CDC offices across the state. Profiles of 12 successful businesses, 19 charge offs and 5 potential losses were analyzed as to the factors that produced success or failure.

Even in a relatively stable economy, however, it is a fact of lending that problems arise and past-due loans occur. When this happens, the borrower is counseled as to possible reasons his business is not prospering. New approaches are discussed and implemented and additional working capital is available if required. If, after all possible assistance and counseling are rendered, there are continuing problems, the borrower may choose one of several alternatives: In some cases he has decided that he is unwilling to attempt any further repayment. In others he has decided to fulfill his obligations even after the business has failed. In either case, collateral pledged against the loan is liquidated to reduce the debt. When the borrower is unwilling to assume any debt remaining the CDC has the choice of either continuing collection against him or accepting the loss. In some cases, extended repayment terms are arranged for the borrower willing to complete his obligation, matched to his ability to repay.

Since its inception, the CDC has financed 251 businesses for an overall investment of $2,803,987. Of those, we have charged off 69 loans, or $855,810 — high by ordinary standards, but the very nature of the program is involvement in high-risk lending. We knew it would be a learning situation for both us and the borrowers and can consider these losses as "research and development" costs. Most importantly, though, close to 200 businesses which might never have been started are now in operation, providing jobs and opportunities where they did not previously exist.

As an extension of our research and development, we have compiled a profile of companies we have financed. This is what we learned (Table 6–1).

The negative results in Table 6–1 point up insufficient performance either by the customer or by CDC; some deficient areas can be attributed to both parties. The following breakdown outlines the strong and weak points of our lending efforts and performance by the businessmen:

1. The Successful Businessman

Provided strong character references
Kept accurate records in every instance
Invested his own money
Provided projections
Had previous banking relationship prior to CDC
Did not have excessive personal indebtedness
Kept personal withdrawals to a minimum
Generally did not employ relatives or friends
Had no history whatsoever of bankruptcy or wage-earner

Showed good job stability prior to CDC
Was extremely cooperative

2. The Unsuccessful Businessman

Could not furnish adequate character references
Did not keep adequate business records
Had little or no personal investment in the business
Generally provided poor or no projections
Had little previous experience in the selected business
Employed relatives or friends in half of failures
Showed a higher percentage of previous bankruptcy or wage-earner
Had little or no banking experience prior to CDC
Indicated very limited previous management experience
Lost interest in the business

3. CDC Performance on Successful Loans

Character references were thoroughly researched
Documented all loans and discussions
Requested and received income projections
Established realistic goals
Received financial statements periodically
Based initial loan approval on character and managerial ability

4. CDC Performance on Unsuccessful Loans

Managerial ability not determined prior to loan
Insufficient character references
Did not require initial income and equipment projections
Generally did not set goals with customer
Poor documentation
Did not require some investment by customer

The findings of the study are already being put to use by our CDC lending officers and advisers, and we believe that, as a result, the positive impact of this lending program will be even greater in the future.

PUBLIC AFFAIRS DEPARTMENT

There is, of course, another side to the Georgia Plan's implementation, that having to do with the citizenship activities of the bank, which were only partially related or totally unrelated to the actual lending function.

One of the things we learned through the original Savannah Plan was that if we were going to be an effective as well as a willing community servant, the initiatives and the programs we undertook had to be centrally coordinated for the entire bank; therefore, in 1970, we formed the Public Affairs Department. Not that this department is the only group that furthers our citizenship objectives—far from it. The Department initiates and coordinates efforts for the entire staff—statewide—of the bank. It was organized with these objectives:

1. Develop a more effective voice in community, state, and national affairs for the bank.

2. Stimulate civic and political activities by informing all staff members, stockholders, directors, legislators, and the general public of the problems facing our community and the bank.

3. Plan and carry out self-help action programs designed to uplift and economically improve the communities in which we operate.

4. Disseminate legislative information and maintain practical legislative liaison.

In summary, the Public Affairs Department is concerned with the bank's complete citizenship responsibilities, which include but are not limited to self-help programs for minority and low-income individuals.

Programs developed to meet this objective have taken a number of forms. As a source of information on issues affecting our bank, customers, stockholders, and the general public, the "Public Affairs Bulletin" was initiated. Rather than attempt surface coverage of several issues at once, each bulletin concentrates on one subject of particular and current interest. Issues are researched and discussed in a question-and-answer format to facilitate reading and ready reference. During 1971, 30,000 copies of a bulletin discussing the Rapid Transit Election in Atlanta were distributed or mailed. During 1972, 12,000 bulletins on low-income housing were distributed. Another 8,000 discussed welfare, and 13,000 covered the issue of drug abuse. In 1973, 15,000 bulletins were distributed concerning the controversial school desegregation plan in Atlanta, and 8,000 more were put out on the issue of "no-fault" insurance which was then before the Georgia legislature.

The Department saw a need to make voter registration more convenient, so, working through the branch administration division in Atlanta, 113 C&S staff members from 60 C&S branches were sworn in as official county registrars. Since the program began in March of 1972, the C&S Bank has registered over 12,000 citizens to vote.

Economic education in the public and secondary schools of the state had long been lacking in emphasis. Through efforts coordinated by the Department, the Georgia Council on Economic Education was organized in 1972. Working through Georgia colleges and businessmen, the Council has begun a statewide program to bring the level of economic education in Georgia schools up to that of other sections of the country. And as a kicker, the bank agreed to underwrite the first three years' expenses of the program.

In 1971, a recreational improvement program called "Spring Swing to Playgrounds" was coordinated by the Department. The undertaking was to provide new playgrounds and upgrade existing playground sites that were neglected mainly as a result of lack of municipal funds. The C&S Bank agreed to match dollar for dollar all money raised by local communities to purchase equipment, and then promised to provide the manpower to assist local groups in assembling the equipment on site.

In Savannah, for example, seven of the 10 banks and savings and loan institutions provided funds and volunteers to build the new playgrounds, and the same type of cooperation emerged in the other cities where the program was offered.

Over $140,000 was raised through the effort. But more importantly, volunteers from churches, schools, civic groups, the U.S. Army, and private businesses erected over 3,500 pieces of equipment in one day across the state, creating 155 new playgrounds—proof again that people can solve their problems on their own when given the proper tools.

In Macon, as with many Georgia cities, dental care among less advantaged families ranged from minimal to none at all. To bring dental care to children of these families, a complete mobile unit was built into a large bus, including three "dentist offices" complete with all necessary equipment. Three fourths of the local dentists volunteered a day of their time on a rotating schedule to staff the bus. A supporting group of dental hygienists and technicians also volunteered their time. The bus visits schools in the area on an established schedule to complete the necessary dental work. Total cost of the mobile unit was approximately $50,000, of which 40 per cent was raised by local schoolchildren selling toothpaste at $1 per tube. The bank and other interested organizations made up the remainder of the cost.

Working through the C&S Bank in Albany, Georgia, a neighborhood library program was established there, providing three new libraries housed in mobile home units. Cards have been issued to over 1000 people—mostly disadvantaged young people. The books are all paperbacks and follow-up on their return has not been too rigid since the scope of the program included an effort to get books into the neighborhood homes. Community assistance has provided such adjuncts as movies, storytelling sessions, and remedial reading programs, all staffed by volunteers. Over 200 children enrolled in the remedial reading classes, which met for six weeks.

In Augusta, a park on the Savannah River was rebuilt and refurnished through the efforts of the bank, other community organizations, civic groups and private citizens. The park is now the scene of an ongoing program of cultural and community activities in which all Augusta area citizens can participate.

In 1973, a program was initiated in two Georgia cities to increase interest and participation in public education by matching bank dollar grants and C&S staff time with "sweat equity" provided by neighborhood school groups. The bank offered to provide the funds of up to $1,000 per school if local parents, teachers, students and other interested groups would develop a plan for an improvement project in each school and match the grant with labor or contribution in equal value. Response to the program was outstanding. Improvements included development of educational nature trails, beautification projects, establishment of audiovisual programs, and expansions of school libraries.

Each of the projects and programs described above was designed to attack a community need and solve it. Each program responded to a different need, but there were some common characteristics. In each case, the bank provided leadership and personnel assistance and agreed to assist in providing the fiscal resources to help get the job done.

TODAY—AND TOMORROW

One problem toward which we are now directing our attention is that of "the individual versus the institutions." Individuals now feeling totally powerless in the face of what they term the "establishment" are relating by negative reactions toward big government and big business. Their reaction has been to join together in small groups to fight it. There is a brighter future for all of us, however, if the establishment can be projected as being human enough to deal with the problems of the community and its citizens over and above their customer service problems. So what we, and others like us, must do is to develop a working relationship with these groups and show them that they can be a part of the "establishment" and thus help direct the changes it brings about.

What will we do this year, or next year? Almost certainly not the same thing we did last year. To continue to be effective in our citizenship undertakings, we must continually redefine the issues in the light of the current situation. Tomorrow's activities might be in the field of women's rights, or they may be rapid transit, or they might be education. Knowing the particular fields is not that important. What is important is that we continue to analyze and stay ahead of the issues and that we react to them constructively as an institution. And to be genuinely constructive, that reaction must continue to be through encouragement of the self-help doctrine, which produces lasting effects, rather than through temporary give-away assistance.

MEASURING THE RESULTS

We've come a long way since 1968, and our method of attacking our citizenship responsibilities has developed from an ad hoc approach into a full-time, carefully planned course of action. As part of our more sophisticated approach, we now feel the time has come to ask ourselves, "How well are we doing our job?" To answer that question, we must find some way to measure the success of our efforts.

Measuring the impact of citizenship activities is not easily accomplished. First, there is the problem of the comparison unit. Although costs may be uniformly expressed in dollars or time, the benefits are quite diverse and incapable of uniform comparison. Second, there has been no agreement as to what constitutes "success" in such long-range undertakings. Thus, at present we have no way of measuring how close we are to it. It is possible, however, to measure how far we have come by setting some definite goals as targets for performance. We can:

1. Devise projects to provide certain agreed-upon results.
2. Estimate cost and time necessary to achieve the results.
3. Compare the performance with goals at regular intervals. This converts the measurement problem in social concerns to a budgetary question, capable of measurement in terms we generally understand.

We are working now to develop a measure or standard of performance to help us better evaluate programs on which we are now spending in excess of $1,000,000 a year. Starting with 1973, we began to maintain information in a form on which we can make comparisons and develop trend information, to see if the dollars we are spending are being effectively directed at our goals.

Much of the development of this technique is still in the future, but we have made a start. The already large investment we're making now in this area continues to grow. If we don't use our managerial skills to follow up in developing a good measurement system, we may deserve the certain criticism now being levied at governmental agencies who simply expend money as a solution to all the needs of society.

In summary, the last five years have been a very satisfying beginning toward fulfilling the most important role the C&S Bank plays—that of corporate citizen. We've done a lot; we're proud of our success and we've learned from our failures—but, more importantly, we've grown in our ability to understand and react. And we hope that maturity will lend added value to our efforts as we continue to approach the issues which confront us.

E. MANDELL DE WINDT

E. Mandell de Windt became Chairman and Chief Executive Officer of Eaton in 1969. His career with the company began in 1941 as a production clerk at Eaton's Valve Division in Battle Creek, Michigan.

Under his direction, Eaton has become a highly diversified global company with sales reaching past the $1.5 billion mark.

A native of Great Barrington, Massachusetts, Mr. de Windt graduated from Berkshire School and attended Williams College. After serving in several personnel assignments, he was named Assistant General Manager of the Stamping Division in 1950, and became general manager in 1953. He was named Assistant Director of Sales for Eaton in 1958, and Vice President-Sales in 1960. A year later, he became Group Vice President-International, and was elected a director in 1964. Mr. de Windt became Executive Vice President in 1967, and was elected President later the same year.

Mr. de Windt is a director of Ohio Bell Telephone, Cleveland Trust, American Can, Diamond Shamrock, Mogul, and Detroit Edison.

As Chairman of United Torch Services, Mr. de Windt has been credited with leading a resurgence of community concern and generosity in Greater Cleveland. He also serves as Vice President and trustee of the Cleveland Clinic. Mr. de Windt is a member of the Board of Governors of United Way of America and serves on the executive committee of the National Conference of Christians and Jews. He is a trustee of Berkshire School, Williams College, Cleveland State University and Cleveland Educational Television.

As a member of the Business Council, the President's Council on Exports, and Industry Policy Advisory Committee for Multilateral Trade Negotiations, Mr. de Windt plays a role in the national economic scene. He is also a director and member of the executive committee of the Greater Cleveland Growth Association. He is a director of the Business-Industry Political Action Committee and a trustee of the U.S. Council, International Chamber of Commerce.

His memberships include: The American Society of Corporate Executives, Society of Automotive Engineers, The Economic Club of New York, The Economic Club of Detroit, and The Society of Cincinnati. He is a Founding Member of the American Friends of Canada.

Among Mr. de Windt's recent awards have been: Commendatore of the Italian Republic, Cleveland's Man of the Year in Business, The Urban League's Businessman Extraordinaire, and the 1973 Human Relations Award of the National Conference of Christians and Jews.

Mr. and Mrs. de Windt are the parents of five children and reside in Lyndhurst, Ohio.

Chapter 7

Close to the Vest Is Close to the Brink

E. MANDELL DE WINDT

Business requires an environment in which to function that is as critical for successful operation as clean air is for breathing. This environment is aptly called the business climate, and it may be good, bad, or indifferent. Right now, it's bad.

Fortunately, however, it's unlike the weather; we *can* do something about it. It's high time that all businessmen recognize the fact and begin to clean up the environment of public opinion—or the business image, if you will—before our companies are choked to death.

Almost a century has passed since a very wealthy businessman replied to a newspaper reporter, "The public be damned." And companies have gradually come to realize that significant benefits can come to them by communicating with the people who are their shareholders and customers, as well as with the public generally. Moreover, laws have been written that require certain disclosures. But some residues of an archaic, better forgotten attitude still prevail in some business circles, causing some companies not necessarily to neglect public opinion, but to pay too little attention to it.

I don't mean to suggest anything sinister in this close-to-the-vest attitude. It may spring simply from a natural and totally understandable love of privacy. It doesn't necessarily imply an unwillingness to be publicly accountable for what is done privately. It may reflect only a feeling that, since the public has no vested interest in the business and no authority to participate in its decisions, the opinion of the public really isn't either useful or important.

More than likely, though, the underlying reason for many businessmen is their own understanding of the free enterprise system, which they regard as so obviously beneficial for all people that they fail to realize how many men and women do not have even the most rudimentary understanding of it. As a consequence, they do not assign to public opinion the tremendous influence that it, in fact, possesses. Their attitude, as a result, arises not from arrogance but from an honest bewilderment that so many people who live in the midst of free enterprise and benefit immensely from it don't even begin to understand it.

Perhaps there was a time when a prevailing business attitude that neglected public opinion was no great disadvantage. But that time has long since passed. The reason is not that business has changed and has grown careless in its efforts to serve its customers. The reason is that public opinion, as an articulate, concerted, well-publicized and well-directed voice in our society, has gained a force far greater than it ever had before. And the winds of discontent are blowing across the land with greater velocity than at any time in our history, threatening, as they do so, to topple even the most fundamental institutions on which our society is built.

This discontent might well be termed a crisis of confidence, and its affects education, government, and even religion as well as business. It reaches to the very roots of the free enterprise system. And in reaching that far, it touches the lives of all Americans.

Every public opinion measuring device points to the same reading on the dial: the confidence barometer is low and falling. A survey of 3,000 students conducted for *U.S. News and World Report* shows that more than half of them felt that United States industry doesn't even want to correct any pollution it may be causing. Opinion Research Corporation reports that 60 per cent of the people it questioned have a low opinion of business in general. Of 9,500 high school students surveyed, more than half believe government ownership of business would be good and should guarantee jobs for everyone willing to work.

Forty-six per cent of the American people agree with the statement: "Big business is dangerous to our way of life." Sixty-eight per cent believe that new Federal laws are needed to protect the consumer, even though more such laws have been passed in the last five years than in the previous 50.

Perhaps the most alarming results of all showed up in two Louis Harris surveys made five years apart. The Harris people took the pulse of confidence of Americans in three of their largest, most fundamental institutions: education, business, and government. Since these institutions are so basic to our way of life, it is essential that people generally have a large measure of confidence in them if they are to continue to operate effectively.

The results for business? In 1966, 58 per cent of the people expressed confidence in business. When the poll was repeated in 1971, that number had fallen to 21 per cent. In other words, only one

American in five really believes in the free enterprise system as it functions in the United States.

It may be helpful to consider why such an attitude has developed. Why, as a matter of fact, do millions of Americans sniff suspiciously about the claims made in advertising, or the quality of products, or the reasons companies give for opposing union demands, or even the figures in corporate news releases?

It wasn't always that way. In the first three decades of this century, people generally had supreme confidence in the ability of business to get things done, to solve problems, and to provide for them the things they want for themselves and their families. Why, when George Romney was a boy, a businessman could even get elected president of the United States!

However, the national confidence got a rude shock when the bottom fell out of the economy and the Great Depression settled down upon us. But that experience is not what brought on the present lack of confidence. We recovered from it and went back to what we knew from experience would work. The man who had sold apples on the street corner opened a grocery store and built up a string of supermarkets that today provide jobs for thousands of people.

The loss of confidence that confronts us today is of much more recent origin. We survived the credibility gap, the missile gap, and the Bay of Pigs—and we came back fighting. Today, something more insidious and more fundamental in its effects seems to be attacking the American spirit.

I am not for a minute suggesting that the disillusionment that has overtaken the American people is groundless. For one thing, it is only necessary to consider the long and frustrating agony of Vietnam to explain much of our dissatisfaction. We were involved in a totally unsatisfactory situation so unwillingly, so helplessly, if you will, and for so long a time that many people simply feel compelled to take action, any kind of action. Unfortunately, that action has often been to merely point the finger of blame at business. Companies are an easy, even an obvious, target. They're big, they're successful, and the protestors and legislators know their addresses.

You can't very well take the same kind of action against other institutions. It is not socially acceptable to throw rocks at a man who is carrying a Bible. That lets religion out. Education escapes because, if you shut down all the schools, you have the kids on your hands all day. And it is still considered unseemly—though less so—to rough up the man who has the American flag draped around his shoulders. That leaves only the big, rich, hard-hearted, mean-minded businessman as the prime target. It's ironical that he can only quote, in defense of his own humanity, the merchant Shylock: "If you cut me, do I not bleed?"

There are other causes of today's dissatisfaction. It's a time when we are advised to be bullish on America, and yet we cannot afford beefsteak. It's a time when we are promised a "Vietnam dividend" at the end of the conflict, and then are told that it has already been spent. It's a time when we thrill with hope at the prospect of trade with Russia, and then find that our taxes were used to subsidize the first sale, and discover the odd agricultural fact that American wheat costs less after a sea voyage to Russia.

It's a time when educational opportunity has been made most widely and most genuinely equal, and the students don't like what they see. It's a time when the economic controls that were supposed to assure the smooth functioning of our industrial machinery have for the most part proved to be monkey wrenches. It's a time when the nation that discovered nuclear fission and nuclear fusion is lining up at gas stations because there is, of all things, an energy shortage. Finally, it's a time when war, the deadliest form of environmental pollution, seems always ready to break out in spite of our most diligent efforts to control it.

And if anyone thinks that Watergate has done anything to help the situation, he would probably be the kind who would compare the Little Big Horn favorably with the Normandy invasion.

So the reasons for dissatisfaction, discontent, and lack of trust are valid enough. What is more to my point, whether or not they are valid, they are a fact. Although it is possible to deplore or even bemoan a fact, it is impossible to deny a fact. It is this hard fact that business must face up to and do something about. It's a matter of survival.

It isn't that businessmen need to be loved by the public. It isn't only that they *like* to be trusted, as all human beings do. It is that they need public confidence if they are to be able to get done the essential work of business. For lack of confidence leads to actions—usually governmental actions—that seriously impair the ability of free enterprise to function effectively.

I sometimes wonder how business in America manages to keep going at all when it has so little public support. Historically, when people lose faith in their institutions, they take steps to get rid of them.

For United States business, it hasn't got to that point—quite. At least, it isn't being done quickly and cleanly. However, the free enterprise system is being drastically changed by a continuing series of restrictions that are like hot, sticky tar on the American road. Where before business sped toward desirable goals, today it can barely slog along. It's a tribute to the innate healthiness of our system that industry still finds the strength to produce so well. How long can it continue?

Business, of itself, is no less enterprising or efficient than it once was. The particular insidiousness of loss of confidence is that it leads to the passage of laws and regulations that tie business up and interfere with its ability to do the job that it is uniquely capable of doing.

When people lose confidence in our business system, they tend to become panicky. Then they turn to their representatives in government to bring about change. They don't necessarily have more confidence in government, but they don't know where else to turn. When Attorney General William Saxbe was a Senator, he commented that many of the politicians of his acquaintance "didn't know enough to chase a chicken downstairs with a broom." Perhaps many Americans feel the same way. However, as they see it, they don't have any alternative except to turn to these politicians, who are only too glad to tinker with the greatest economic system ever devised by man.

Public opinion is the grist of the political mill. If the public is soured on business, the politicians will treat businessmen as a natural enemy. They will "color their hats black" and chase them out of town — if they are convinced that that is what their constituents want. That's why businessmen, who have learned from experience the totally unique values of the free enterprise system, have to be concerned with public opinion.

If American public opinion were overwhelmingly in favor of business, then I believe our lawmakers would accord it the same cooperative treatment that the governments of Japan and the European countries accord their business establishments. In those countries, business enterprise is encouraged, honored, and assisted. Their legislators realize that they are on the same team as the businessmen when it comes to achieving desirable social and economic goals for the nation.

My effort in making these observations is not to arouse anyone to righteous anger against politicians; it would be more fitting to take a leaf from their book — to fight fire with fire. If they have become empowered to tinker with a system that has brought such a high standard of living to America, it is because they know how to recognize and respond to public opinion. An elder statesman from Virginia, Henry Gilmer, said it all when he said, "The first law of political leadership is to find out where the people want to go, and then take credit for leading them there." Unfortunately, where they want to go today is on the road to putting more restrictions on the business system in which they have lost confidence. It's up to businessmen to turn public opinion around.

Businessmen are not running for office, that's true. But in a sense they are running for their lives. Unlike most political campaigns, however, fighting to save the free enterprise system is not merely a self-serving campaign. It is not simply an effort to save one's company or one's own position. It is pre-eminently a campaign to preserve the American way of life, of which the free enterprise system is at once a natural outgrowth, an essential part, and a firm foundation.

As we approach the two-hundredth anniversary of our country, it would be a serious lack if our celebration did not include a fresh declaration of confidence in the free enterprise system, which has proved such a strong safeguard of freedom both for our nation and for us as individuals. It would be tragic if we were to allow that cornerstone of freedom to erode. It would be equally tragic if businessmen did not show as much courage and determination in working for the essential economic freedom they need as our ancestors showed when they were drawn up against a powerful empire.

At the same time, I confess to some bewilderment. How can anyone presume to tinker with an economic system that has, for so many years, gone on from success to success? Who would try to change Hank Aaron's batting style? To what would he change it?

Does Socialism provide the answer, even looked at merely from the economic point of view? In the United Kingdom today, one massive strike follows another; in fact, a strike by a labor union has led to the downfall of the government. Strikes have disrupted the very warp and woof of life in England and have put practically a whole country out of work. And the government, set up with the noble purpose of protecting the worker against individual entrepreneurs, who are presumed to be greedy, is in the position of denying pay increases to hundreds of thousands of its citizens.

If all American industry were nationalized, what would the effects on it be of such events as Watergate or the resignation of the President or Vice President? Some years ago, the sordid Profumo scandal rocked the English government to its foundations. What can workers think when their employers—which is what the government becomes in a Socialist state—betray their trust in any way? A scandal in that kind of economy does not merely affect the price of a single company's stock; it profoundly shakes the whole industrial structure.

Could anyone who has enjoyed the healthy state of checks and balances provided by competition in a free economy really prefer a system in which competition is eliminated, bureaucrats wrap their dubious presents to citizens in red tape, and the local "disc jockey," from the mere fact that he has been elected or appointed to office, assumes economic responsibilities comparable to those of the Chairman of the Board of General Motors?

If Socialism isn't the answer, what does Communism offer, on economic grounds alone, that would make it preferable to free enterprise? All that we know of the quality of life in the Soviet Union indicates that Communism is simply incapable of providing for its people what free enterprise does so consistently and almost casually. Central authority discourages private initiative, which looms large in all human beings as a motivating force, no matter what their political and cultural heritage. And the stronger the central authority, the weaker a nation becomes, because it simply fails to make use of the individual talents of so many of its citizens.

One day in 1927, Mrs. Charles Kettering mentioned to her husband, the great electrical inventor, a newspaper account that a young man named Charles Lindbergh had just flown across the ocean alone. "Well," replied Mr. Kettering, "I'm sure he didn't do it by committee." That comment, perhaps as much as anything, sums up the inherent weakness of the Communist economic system.

But I don't think I need to belabor the point that, after 50 years of five-year plans and ten-year plans and innumerable experiments, Communism has failed to provide its people with anything approaching the standard of living that we who live in a free economy take for granted.

I should like to acknowledge that it is, of course, impossible to validly dismiss two kinds of economy, under which millions live, in so few words as I have used. At the same time, I do not think that any profound analysis is required to determine that the batting averages of Socialism and Communism do not put them in the same league with free enterprise.

Would a satisfactory alternative, then, be a restricted free enterprise, with phases and regulatory agencies and government-mandated specifications on thousands of products? That might make some sense, *if* the government manufactured products, and designed and engineered and marketed them as well; *if* the government undertook the risk that free enterprise of its nature involves; *if* the government rose or fell on its ability to satisfy customers; and, above all, *if* the government had the expertise and the risk capital required to do the job.

You know, some of the things that politicians do would be amusing if they were not so likely to produce tragic consequences. The Food and Drug Administration would land with both feet on any drug manufacturer who distributed drugs before they were thoroughly tested and thoroughly proved. And so they should—nobody should be allowed to endanger the health of the American people.

But these same politicians blithely set in motion so-called remedies—no matter how untested or unproven—that can endanger the very life of the economic system on which we all depend. They are allowed to do so because the public has come to cast a suspicious eye on business—and the reason for that is because they are engulfed with misinformation about business profits and practices—or no information at all—because too many businessmen are content to sit back and not take the real story of business to people who otherwise would have no contact with it.

I am aware that businessmen have many other matters to claim their attention: new products, new plants, labor negotiations, effective marketing strategy, and a host of other things. As the man said, when you're knee-deep in alligators, it's hard to remember that your original purpose was to drain the swamp. But none of those things will matter if business is not free to bring them about. And it will only be free when businessmen keep ever before their fellow-citizens the benefits *to them* of the free enterprise system.

What's more, no businessman can afford to "let George do it." Some businessmen I know apparently have decided that, among any representative group, there will, on average, be enough other people to take the business story to the people. However, this is so big a job that no one group of persons, no one company, nor even any one association of companies can do the job alone.

Also, it is well to remember what Bobby Bragan, who used to manage the old Milwaukee Braves, once said about people who play the averages. "Suppose," he said, "you are standing with one foot in a bonfire and the other in a bucket of ice. According to the averages, you should be perfectly comfortable."

So it is risky to put any blind faith in averages. The only way to be sure the job gets done is for each businessman to do it himself. If that puts him above the average, so much the better.

It seems to me that this is a particularly promising time for businessmen to speak out. There are those who might say that, because of the energy crisis, they should lie low—or, as Madison Avenue likes to put it, maintain a low profile. After all, they say, the crisis has stirred up additional criticism of business for failing to head off the shortage, then compounding matters by trying to benefit from it through excessive prices and profits.

That's one point of view, but I disagree with it—for several reasons. For one thing, it has become apparent that, in this crisis, business is as much a victim as the individual. When hundreds of thousands of workers are laid off, that's not merely a difficult blow for them; it also means a big step backward for the companies that employ them. And, while the workers have the blow cushioned by unemployment insurance and other benefits, the companies have no such cushion. That's a part of the story that needs to be told, even though it appears that people are already beginning to have some vague realization of it.

Another reason I disagree is that, in spite of the lack of confidence in business they profess, people are turning more and more to business for the solution. They seem to realize that government cannot produce anything; at best, it can regulate. In a recent interview, Senator Barry Goldwater put the whole matter well, when he said: "All we've done [on Capitol Hill] hasn't put one gallon of gaso-line in anybody's tank. Nobody's gone out and started drilling new holes. So far, all we've been arguing about in the Senate is how to impose regulations and create new staffs and new bureaus and add to the woes of people who are honestly trying to get more fuel for the American people."

What the Senator capsulized, the people recognize. Apparently, the successes of the past 200 years of free enterprise haven't been lost on them. They are still able to distinguish between the producers and the regulators — and they know which to turn to in an emergency. Let's hope that that instinct, deep-bred in the American spirit, never deserts us. But let's do more than hope. It's time for business to take the lead.

I do not blame politicians for their inability to make up shortages. That's not their job. They are not equipped for it. *But business is.* That's what it is most capable of doing. And now, while the iron is hot, is the time for businessmen to assume the leadership that they have too long let go by default. The American people are looking for strong, effective leadership in this emergency, leadership that can *do* something, that can produce.

Once there was an old country doctor, who was consulted by a patient whose disease he could not identify in spite of his best efforts. Not wanting to lose the patient's confidence, he asked, "Tom, have you ever had this before?" "Yes, doc, I have," said the man. "Well," said the doctor, "you've got it again."

Political officials are often like that when they bump up against economic matters. They may know something is wrong, but they don't know what it is and haven't an idea in the world how to cure it. The people who, from actual experience, know and appreciate the free enterprise system are the ones best equipped to cure its ills. Businessmen today can't simply do the job and let it go at that. They have to let people know they *are* doing the job, and remind them that, in our system, this is the way we have to proceed.

At Eaton, we think this is so important a part of our duties as businessmen and managers of a corporation that, about a year and a half ago, we set up a program to insure that it gets done con-sistently and well. We call the program Comm/Pro and it is designed to take the business story to people who ordinarily do not hear it. We believe that this is the way to work toward restoring confidence in business and the business system, to the extent that one company can help to turn the tide.

When we came to realize what loss of confidence was doing to United States business, we set about rebuilding confidence. And since the weakening of confidence came from failure to communi-cate effectively, we set ourselves to the task of communicating. A survey of our assets for the task revealed that we had, right in the company, the best group of free enterprise communicators to be found anywhere—people who knew the system, who believed in it, and who had seen it work because they had helped to make it work. Those people are our own top managers.

Beginning with the Chairman of the Board, every Eaton officer was given the opportunity to mouth his views on his livelihood. Altogether, about 125 people were recruited through "executive invitation," a method many may first have encountered from their Army sergeant.

We appointed a national coordinator, whose responsibility it is to publicize the program and to ferret out audiences. The audiences are there, if you know where to look for them. Rotary, Kiwanis, and Lions Clubs alone hold more than two million meetings a year across the length and breadth of the land. Parents assemble at more than 45,000 PTA meetings every month. Teachers, government employees, and local unions also provide important audiences.

And these are people we want to talk to, people who rarely participate in a business discussion and who may never have met a real, live businessman. When we ran ads in the Cleveland and Detroit newspapers inviting people to "Spend an Hour with a Capitalist," many groups decided to do just that.

We have had a very satisfying experience since we turned into hucksters for business. In the past year, we have addressed hundreds of audiences and thousands of people. They are receptive and friendly. They may propose some hard questions in the Questions and Answers sessions. But all in all, they are glad to meet you, grateful that you have taken time to visit with them, and for the most part are not as hostile toward business when the dialogue is over.

Through radio, television, and newspaper coverage, we have learned to extend ourselves. Recently, one of our scientists in Michigan held a phone conference with a high school class in Hudson, Ohio. We have been invited to several Career Days in just the second year of our program. The Cleveland Public School system, this year alone, has scheduled Comm/Pro speakers for 140 groups of students. And our experience has been so satisfactory that we recently began training Eaton management in Canada as spokesmen for business.

Of course, Eaton cannot even begin to do the whole job by itself. It would be ridiculous for us to pretend that we are the designated pinch hitter for all of industry. We need solid hitters all the way through the line-up. The very survival of our business system depends on public opinion. Right now, public opinion is being formed by politicians, labor unions, economics professors, bureaucrats, environmentalists, and the Ralph Naders of the world. They are spreading the word about business while we are sitting on the sidelines—and the word they are spreading is usually about four letters long. People are willing to listen to us and to believe us. We have found that out through our Comm/Pro presentations. These presentations are needed, and they are effective. What more do businessmen need to get going?

When I was a boy, I had to memorize a poem about the boy who stood on the burning deck and managed to keep cool while everyone else was working like mad to put out the flames. At that time, we were taught to admire the young man for his composure. Since then, I wonder. There's a time when action is the only answer. I believe that a businessman who keeps silent today is like that boy; unless he swings into action, his ship is going to go down in flames.

It certainly seems ironic to me that so many businessmen are overconfident of the ability of the business system to survive while four in five Americans have lost confidence in it. They have proved themselves the best salesmen in all the world. They have peddled everything from hula hoops to jet aircraft. They have sold stocks and bonds and health insurance and intangibles like the United Foundation. And yet, when the big blue chips are down, when business is being attacked right on its home ground, it seems to fold up. Any little Campfire Girl does a better job selling her cookies than most businessmen have done selling the greatest economic system ever devised by man.

It's time now for them to sweep the length and breadth of this land with the business story, the true business story, the story of accomplishment, of social concern, of sensitivity to customers' needs, of responsible citizenship. They must sweep away the myths of 28 per cent profits, lack of concern about pollution, and a to-hell-with-the-customer attitude. They must tell people where the 85 million jobs in this country really come from; who pays the taxes that finance our hospitals and schools and social programs; who lays a foundation of security for so many millions of workers and their families; who erects the greatest, most powerful safeguard to their freedom, which is economic freedom.

It will be a tough fight, but the prize is worth the pressure. For when all businessmen act together to reestablish confidence in American business, they can set the world on its ear.

On my first trip to Washington many years ago, I was riding in a cab past the National Archives. Over the doorway were inscribed the words, "What is past, is prologue." As I was squinting at the lettering, the cab driver said, "Mister, that means, 'You ain't seen nothing yet.' "

That's what business can do when it stops playing it close to the vest and carries forth the business story as energetically and imaginatively as it has marketed its products.

ARTHUR R. TAYLOR

Arthur R. Taylor was elected President and a Director of CBS in 1972. Since that time, he has been an outstanding spokesman in the communications industry and a leading corporate advocate of increased business involvement in major social issues.

Mr. Taylor was named CBS President after a remarkable and diverse career in the academic and business worlds, where he excelled first as a scholar and then quickly earned a reputation as a brilliant financial analyst noted for his aggressive and innovative approaches to management.

Born in Rahway, New Jersey, on July 6, 1935, Mr. Taylor graduated from Rahway High School in 1953. He attended Brown University on a full-tuition scholarship, graduating in 1957 with a Bachelor of Arts degree magna cum laude in Renaissance history. He also was elected to Phi Beta Kappa. Intending to pursue an academic career, Mr. Taylor worked as an admissions officer at Brown to finance further studies, and earned a Master of Arts degree in American economic history in 1961.

While researching his master's thesis on Samuel Insull, a tycoon whose financial empire collapsed in the 1929 stock market crash, Mr. Taylor became fascinated with the world of finance. In 1961, he joined The First Boston Corporation as a trainee. Advancing rapidly, he was named a Vice President in 1966 and a Director of First Boston in 1969. In 1970, Mr. Taylor joined the International Paper Company as Vice President-Finance, and reorganized the company's financial structure. When he left International Paper to join CBS, he was Executive Vice President, Chief Financial Officer, a Director, and a member of the Executive Committee.

Mr. Taylor has moved boldly and decisively at CBS, streamlining the corporate structure, divesting it of marginal activities, acquiring promising new ventures and strengthening existing operations. He also has established himself as a vigorous and outspoken champion of a free press and opponent of government interference in broadcasting.

When he joined CBS, Mr. Taylor told an interviewer: "I think a free, strong communications system is an absolute necessity to the functioning of society. I think it's right at the heart of society." Since then, Mr. Taylor has taken the lead in speaking out against government encroachment on broadcasters' freedoms. He has fought vigorously against attempts by government agencies to use regulatory procedures to impose government control on broadcasting. He has similarly defended the freedom of print journalists, as well as those of broadcast journalists.

Mr. Taylor also has been active in extending and broadening the public's access to events through broadcasting. It was his Congressional testimony, along with that of other broadcast executives, as well as Mr. Taylor's telegram to Congressional leaders, that led up to the decision to open to broadcasting key sessions of the 1974 Presidential Impeachment proceedings, which added significantly to public understanding of the process.

With his liberal academic background and broad range of interests, Mr. Taylor is on the cutting edge of the emerging generation of American business leaders—businessmen who are seeking new corporate directions and a deeper corporate commitment to the larger questions of society. "The President of a firm such as CBS," he has said, "has to be concerned with social and political questions. He can no longer be just an operating head; those days are past. Corporations today need a generalist." He calls upon his fellow businessmen to be more receptive not only to "unorthodox ideas—but, most importantly, to unorthodox people."

Mr. Taylor believes that business, to remain a vital force in society, must compete more effectively for talented people. To do this, corporations must see to it that business careers are as exciting and rewarding as careers in the arts, in public service, or in the academic world. "The job of those who have achieved leadership positions is to magnify the dignity of those around them, not their own," he

states. Under Mr. Taylor's direction, CBS has taken far-reaching, affirmative steps to improve the opportunities in the Company for youth, women, and minorities.

Mr. Taylor has maintained his close association with the academic and intellectual community. His active speaking schedule includes many appearances on college campuses, and he is a trustee of both Brown University and Bucknell University. Mr. Taylor also maintains a strong interest in foreign affairs. He is a member of the Council on Foreign Relations, a trustee of The Asia Society, a Commissioner of the Trilateral Commission, and Director of the Japan Society.

Chapter 8

Generating Light

ARTHUR R. TAYLOR

Long before other American businesses were directly engaged in battle for basic rights, one particular American business was confronted with the need to stand up and fight for freedom.

The embattled business was journalism, almost two and a half centuries ago, and the case in question involved John Peter Zenger, a printer who was publishing a newspaper in colonial New York City. The people who bought his paper looked to him for information. And when he was candid about the Royal Governor, the British government prosecuted him for libel.

It was that case, tried in 1735, that established the first basic right of free journalism. Zenger was acquitted because of the truth of what he had published.

In the long procession of time since a Philadelphia lawyer named Andrew Hamilton won Zenger's freedom and began the protection of journalism against government prosecution, the independence of news reporting has become a major tool of self-government, and news honestly reported has become a major element in the American society.

The role of the press as part of the process of self-government is historic. President Washington's Farewell Address first reached the public in the pages of the *Philadelphia Daily American Advertiser;* President Franklin D. Roosevelt's proclamation of a national bank holiday was conveyed to every corner of the nation instantly via commercial radio. Presidential candidates Kennedy and Nixon met in televised debate and the largest percentage of voter participation in a Presidential election came that very year.

Increasingly through the years the public has come to regard broadcasting as its most reliable and most immediate source of news. Increasingly, broadcast journalism has become not only a major functional obligation but also a major business activity for broadcasters. And of all the broadcaster's business activities, journalism is the one which requires the most constant and vigilant defense of its liberty.

The defense of freedom and liberty is sometimes assumed to be the special domain of the underprivileged and the dispossessed. This is an assumption which defies history. It is sometimes noted that George Washington was one of the richest men in the colonies, yet he chose to lead the American Revolution. Certainly it is a fact that there have been no more devoted defenders of freedom than those in the business of broadcast journalism — because freedom, in a very real sense, is so essential to broadcast journalism in our society.

And so it is that a profit-making entity such as CBS, throughout its history, has been in the forefront of the battle for journalistic freedom for the broadcaster.

At CBS we are particularly fortunate in having had one man consistently at the helm throughout the course of this continuing endeavor. William S. Paley has played a key part in defining the role of broadcast journalism and in the defense of its essential rights. This has been an effort spanning decades, linking generations, and encompassing basic principles of the United States concept of government.

Back in 1933, when newspapers and wire services, seeing in giant young radio a new and redoubtable competitor for public attention, tried to cut off service to broadcasters, it was Mr. Paley who established the Columbia News Service and showed that CBS was prepared to conduct its own newsgathering and news reporting operations.

When the news wire services restored radio to their list of clients, broadcasters were not long content to place their entire reliance in such service, and during World War II the broadcasts of such CBS News correspondents as Edward R. Murrow gave broadcast news an immediacy unique up to that time in the annals of American journalism.

But as broadcast news developed — and even before the advent of television magnified its impact and its organizational size — it faced the constant problem of preserving its freedom.

The print press existed at the time of the framing of the Constitution, and the First Amendment specifically guarantees freedom of the press. The idea of licensing newspapers, though occasionally proposed, has always been defeated by the basic guarantee of press freedom enacted in 1791 in the First Amendment, and tracing back in its philosophical origins to John Peter Zenger. The idea of licensing broadcast stations, however, was enacted into law because the broadcast spectrum is limited and two stations cannot broadcast on the same frequency in the same area.

Licensing was, historically, a physical necessity. And since there was and is competition for broadcast licenses, the government was charged with setting standards for the granting of these valuable permissions to broadcast.

Ever since that function was assumed by the government, there has been contention between where licensing ends and censorship begins. News is and always has been a principal stock in trade of the broadcaster. News by its very nature often involves the reporting of differences, the selection of topics for reportage, the choice of reporters. Particularly since so much news involves the activities of government and the discovery and dissemination of facts, the people have a right to know about what their government is doing. Broadcast journalism — by its very nature — occupies something of an adversary position, regardless of what party or what administration happens to be in power at the moment. Conscientious broadcast journalism constantly reports events and views on which there are wide differences of opinion, and wide degrees of opposing passions.

News and documentary broadcasts are presented generally as part of a broad schedule of entertainment and informational programming. In the United States the audience has more choice between channels and more diversity than any other nation on earth. That is because our system of broadcasting is both competitive and profit-oriented. Every broadcaster in the commercial marketplace survives or fails on the degree to which he attracts the attention of the audience. In this regard, news broadcasts are as competitive as entertainment offerings. They compete for the attention of the audience — the attention born of confidence in what is being watched.

This competition exists on both the network and local station levels. It is competition for viewers, competition to provide the best news service.

The nature of the broadcasting business makes CBS — and other broadcasters — conscientious and vigilant in defense of freedom. CBS is a corporation which takes its public interest responsibility most seriously. CBS owned stations and the hundreds of independently owned stations affiliated with the CBS Radio and Television Networks are all licensed in the public interest, convenience, and necessity. Whereas many companies, particularly those whose activities are subjected in some degree to the approval of regulatory agencies, have decided that the best policy is invisibility and tend to avoid issues that might irritate legislators or regulators, news gatherers and news reporting must by definition seek out the core of public controversy. It is there that the news occurs, and it is there the reporter must go if he is to give the audience the story of what is occurring.

Inevitably, those who are part of the news—particularly high government officials who figure repeatedly in the news—will from time to time be displeased with the way their actions or positions are reported. Most recently, this was true of the Watergate affair from the very first reports. The fact that one aspect after another was brought to light through the efforts of journalists did not in the least discourage attempts to restrict journalistic coverage thereafter.

Given such circumstances, it might be thought that a broadcasting company would be well advised to minimize the kind of news activity which could provoke the displeasure that leads to efforts to limit press freedom. But CBS has never operated that way. If we had, we would not have maintained so consistent an effort, through the years, to protect and expand the freedom of broadcast journalism.

It is important to explain some of the reasons why CBS gives the highest priority to the maintenance of an active and professional news operation.

The first fundamental assumption of management thinking at CBS is that the full and free transmission of news is absolutely essential to the functioning of our democracy, our society, our economy, and our nation.

Our founding fathers incorporated the same belief into the Constitution in the form of the First Amendment; they were convinced from the beginning that only a fully informed electorate could adequately fulfill the responsibilities of a democracy, and that only a free and unfettered press could provide the necessary flow of information. Adam Smith, who set out the basic principles of a free economy, similarly made the informed consumer a prerequisite to the effective functioning of such an economy. To put this another way, in 1960 President Eisenhower's Commission on National Goals identified 11 "goals at home" toward which the nation should strive. They were: maximum individual freedom, equality of opportunity, perfection of the democratic process, strengthening of education, advancement of the arts and sciences, diffusion of economic power, fostering of economic growth, planning for technological change, re-establishing free markets for agriculture, improving urban planning and housing, and extending health services. It can readily be seen that each of these goals is served by, and might be impossible to achieve without, the flow of information which the news process provides. Today, other goals would probably be added to such a list—for example, insuring that government officials fulfill their public obligations to sustain the confidence of the electorate.

The second assumption is that within the spectrum of the news media, broadcast news has a very special and important function to perform. Newspapers and magazines constituted the free press long before radio or television was dreamed of; they still perform services broadcasters can neither duplicate nor imitate. But the immediacy and vitality of broadcasting gives it an equally unique role. It is one thing to read about an event after it has occurred; it is quite another to hear about it as it is occurring; and it is still another to see it as it occurs. One need only ask anyone over the age of 20 or 25 where he was during the 48 hours following the assassination of President John F. Kennedy. Almost certainly, the answer will be that he or she was somewhere near a radio or television set. In the weeks following that tragedy, praise for the broadcast coverage of the events in Dallas and Washington was widespread and warm; the common theme was that the coverage had pulled the nation together at a time when hysteria and fear could have caused international chaos.

But the landmarks of broadcast journalism go back half a century before the 1963 tragedy in Dallas. Reporting of the news was one of the first great functions approached by broadcasters when the era of broadcasting began. The election returns of 1920 came over the air to early home radio listeners and a new age of public information was born. By 1924, listeners in many cities heard the tense proceedings of the Democratic National Convention broadcast from Madison Square Garden in New York, with the refrain repeated at the start of most of the 104 ballots: "Alabama casts 24 votes for Oscar W. Underwood." For a long time thereafter this familiar announcement became a standard popular catchphrase.

The government of the United States is a people's government, dependent on the people's choices. It has been that way since the very beginning, with a steady expansion of the eligible electorate.

When our founding fathers wrote the Constitution of the United States, they created three separate branches of government—Legislative, Executive, and Judicial—each with powers to check and balance the others. And they gave to the people a power to check up on all three, through the press that would be beholden to no one. The First Amendment of our Constitution says "Congress shall make no law respecting an establishment of religion, or prohibiting the free exercise thereof; or abridging the freedom of speech, or of the press; or the right of the people peaceably to assemble, and to petition the government for a redress of grievances."

Using that freedom, news media have made it possible for all the people in our country to see at firsthand some of the fundamental processes of our government and the challenges posed, confronted, or evaded by those in positions of high responsibility.

Just as the highest officials of our government have a sworn duty to uphold and enforce the Constitution, we in the news media have a duty to report fully, fairly, and impartially how those officials perform their duty.

If Watergate, for example, was a challenge to our government, it was equally a challenge to the press. If members of the press had not had the courage to report the story, and to stand by it under attack from the highest levels of government, the story might quickly have been forgotten. The result would have been a far greater tragedy for this country—the institutionalization of illegality in the nation's capital.

It is important to note that broadcast journalism had not one but two roles in the unraveling of Watergate. Like reports for newspapers and magazines, broadcast journalists participated in investigating and reporting the basic facts. But it was also broadcast journalism that, early on, pointed its cameras at the Ervin Committee and its witnesses and, in so doing, first brought the whole affair to life for millions upon millions of Americans. There were those who said we should not have done so, but it is my belief that the immediacy of these broadcasts, as much as any other single element, brought home to the American people the nature of what happened under the name of Watergate, and so insured that the same American people will never allow anything like Watergate to happen again.

Before the advent of television, this might not have been the case. When we consider the responsibilities of a broadcaster within a rapidly changing society, we must begin by acknowledging that broadcasting is one of the reasons it is a rapidly changing society. In the United States in the twentieth century, only the automobile can rival television for the impact it has had on the average American family. The auto extended a man's legs until he could span a continent in a matter of days. Television extended his eyes until he could literally see around the world instantly, and beyond.

Consider where television has taken us in recent years. When a man set foot on the moon scores of millions of people watched him do it. A President was assassinated; within minutes television was there, and more millions watched appalled as the suspected assassin was himself assassinated. A President spoke to a nation, and stunned it with his decision not to run for office again. For a century, war had been something Americans went off to, not something that came home to them. Television brought the face of war in Vietnam into every living room in the country.

By opening the eyes of the mass audience radio had gathered, television had other, less dramatic but equally significant effects. Names like Nikita Khrushchev and Kwame Nkrumah became figures Americans had actually seen and heard. Oceans and jungles were explored without leaving one's home. Zurich and Calcutta became backgrounds almost as familiar as Los Angles and Boston. Eventually, social scientists will gauge precisely what effect these aspects of television have had; for myself, I cannot help but believe that their influence has been pervasive.

There was a time, more than a century ago, when a citizen who had the money and didn't mind a month's travel could go to Washington, personally observe every agency of his nation's government in action, and top off the day with a chat with the President of the United States.

Today, thanks to broadcasting, all citizens can hear major government officials discuss their activities, and hear them questioned on their actions by members of the press. With television a President can account for his stewardship in office to an entire nation at a moment's notice, and if he does not do so from time to time, the American people are now accustomed to asking why. I do not believe it an accident that the average citizen's knowledge of his government, his society, and his world have increased so dramatically during the era of broadcasting.

Accessibility is only one ingredient of the impact of broadcasting. Credibility is another, and in many ways it is the more important of the two. From our beginnings, we have felt that the trust which the American people reposed in us was the most vital measure of our success. The broadcasting industry, and CBS individually, have on several occasions commissioned major surveys to study audience attitudes toward our efforts. The most recent ones, like their predecessors, report that television is the most used, and the most trusted, news medium in the nation. I do not wish to belabor this matter, but let me share one item from a study performed by the Roper Organization. That 1972 study found that 64 per cent of the American people relied on television for most of their news, and that 48 per cent of the populace found television more believable than any other news medium.

Such trust does not spring from the wizardry of modern electronics. It is the trust an audience grants to those media that uphold traditional principles of responsible journalism. More than three quarters of a century ago, Adolph Ochs, publisher of *The New York Times,* defined his task: "To give the news impartially, without fear or favor, regardless of any party, sect or interest involved." The Scripps-Howard newspapers put it this way—"Give light, and the people will find their own way."

That is still the job—to generate light. There are times when that mission can be accomplished to an almost uniformly favorable response. Such an experience occurred when the nation's television and radio networks broadcast four debates between John F. Kennedy and Richard M. Nixon, the two principal candidates for the U.S. Presidency in 1960. Later, one of those men called the broadcasts "a great service to the American people." The other called it "a public service of the highest order." I leave it to you to determine which quotation comes from the winner of the election, and which from the loser.

There is a law of physics, however, that tells us light is often accompanied by heat. We have found this to apply to broadcasting as well!

There are those who think it would somehow be better if television, the most graphic of the news media, were to gloss over on-the-scene realities of war or human suffering; I do not agree. The greatest deterrent to war is the first-hand knowledge of what war is like. If television has helped impart some of that knowledge to the American people, I cannot regret it.

Similarly, we are told that television has created a new breed of politician, photogenic and charming but lacking in substance. I would argue that exactly the opposite is true. For as long as politics has existed, there have been politicians who capitalized on charm. By repeatedly showing these people to all their constituents, television vastly increases their opportunity to demonstrate their real strengths and weaknesses.

Nevertheless, these issues point the way to the central problem, and the central responsibility, of broadcasting as it exists today in the United States. The growth of our society has been accompanied by an even more rapid growth in the number of voices that wish to be heard within it. There is a television set — or, in many cases, more than one set — in virtually every home in our country. Those sets are in use, on the average, more than six hours a day. Because the medium is so pervasive, and so well regarded, it is constantly besieged by those who wish it to carry their particular message. We are asked to discuss one thing, to advocate another, to ignore a third. We are constantly asked to stress one theme, or ban another, in our entertainment programs.

If there were a thousand hours in a day, it might be theoretically possible to accommodate all the demands made upon us. But even if there were, we would not do so. The best newspapers learned, long before television existed, that to say "yes" to any one special interest, no matter how sincere or powerful, is to make it impossible to say "no" to a hundred others of equal sincerity and importance. It is a Pandora's box we have thought it best never to open.

And so our principle has always been that we will listen to all voices, that we will use our best judgment to select what we think most worthy of the attention of our audience. We will not be swayed by any other interest, no matter whose it is. We expect to be judged by what we broadcast; if we do our job responsibly, we believe we will be in tune with our audience far more often than we are out of tune.

When we are out of tune, we learn about it very quickly. There are four television networks and over 900 individual television stations competing for the attention of American audiences. The American viewer's loyalty is of short life. If he ceases to believe in, or to enjoy, what he sees on one television channel, he quickly switches to another; if there is nothing he finds suitable, he simply turns off his television set. When he does, audience surveys tell us about it almost immediately. I think the clearest evidence that we are doing something right is that every year, the average television set in the average American home is used a little more than it was the year before.

The United States is a better country today because we have not been afraid to demand and confront the truth, no matter how unpleasant it occasionally may be, no matter how difficult it may be to find. The news story which television conveys with every passing day is that a free people in the United States are determined to maintain their freedom, to see for themselves, to know what is going on. For as long as broadcasting exists, this will be its highest responsibility.

Having said all that, I would like to be able to add that everyone is in complete agreement with the principles by which we conduct ourselves and that we find the environment in which we operate wholly satisfactory. But, at any moment, we are likely to find ourselves confronted with a multitude of challenges.

For example, we think the country would benefit from changes in the laws of our land so that we may again broadcast debates between major political candidates, as we did in 1960. At the same time, we oppose the idea of compulsory and concentrated preemptions of programs to accommodate myriad candidates in a clutter of political broadcasts that would, in a very real sense, turn the television viewer off. We are hopeful of changes in the rules of our Congress, so that we may be free to cover *any* proceedings of major public importance, not just an occasional committee hearing or special subject. We have actively supported legislation that would assure the privacy of news reporters' notes and sources, thereby protecting those newsmen from the inhibiting effect of subpoenas and compulsory revelation of unpublished information.

I do not believe that the people who differ with us in these and other matters are consciously setting out to eliminate broadcasting's freedom of expression. I am sure that most of them are trying to further causes they consider to be in the best interests of the nation and our modern society.

Regardless of motivation, however, the fact remains that demands for access to broadcast time for one purpose or another recur regularly as an issue, not merely between public officials and broadcasters, but also between broadcasters and those whose view of proper broadcast policy differs. One such case arose in mid-1974 when the Mobil Oil Corporation, on the heels of the fuel crisis, sought to buy time on the networks for "idea advertising" on public issues. Mobil said it wanted to buy the time because broadcast news coverage had not been adequate. It may be of interest to reproduce here the substance of the letter I wrote to editors (July 10) in response to Mobil's heavy publicity for its complaint.

TO EDITORS:
Should broadcasters be forced to sell advertising time to partisan interests for special pleading on controversial matters of public policy? The United States Supreme Court has said no. Speaking for the majority in ruling on that very issue last year, Chief Justice Burger wrote that "the public interest . . . would scarcely be served by a system so heavily weighted in favor of the financially affluent, or those with access to wealth."

This point is precisely what is at the heart of the CBS rejection of a bid by Mobil Oil Corporation to buy commercial broadcast time to promote Mobil's position regarding controversial energy issues. Only a year after the Supreme Court ruled in CBS's favor, Mobil has undertaken a campaign against what it calls "the networks' rejection of idea advertising." Mobil contends that the principle at stake is the First Amendment's protection of freedom of speech.

The opposite is the case, however. What is at stake is that other cardinal provision of the First Amendment: freedom of the press. That was the basis of the Supreme Court's 1973 ruling in *Columbia Broadcasting System, Inc. vs. Democratic National Committee.* There, the Court refused to compel broadcasters to sell advertising air time to groups seeking to present their views on public issues. The High Court upheld the validity of the principle under which CBS and many other broadcasters have had long-standing policies that prohibit the sale of advertising time for the presentation of points of view on controversial issues of public importance, except in the case of certain political broadcasts.

The reason that CBS adopted this policy many years ago was simply that broadcast advertising time is limited—unlike newspaper advertising space or the number of pamphlets that a partisan can distribute. To permit this time to be purchased for propaganda purposes, other than certain political advertising, would mean that those with the most money would get to talk the loudest. It would deluge the airwaves with viewpoints whose claim to broadcast time would be based purely on the ability of their proponents to purchase time for their espousal. It was in recognition of this principle that CBS in the past has turned down the editorial advertisements of many organizations other than Mobil: the Democratic National Committee, the AFL-CIO, numerous oil companies, and other major corporations.

Partisans generally feel that their particular views do not receive enough attention in normal journalistic channels, and that is the case here. CBS is aware that the exigencies of the energy crisis have placed Mobil and others involved in difficult positions explaining their policies to the public. CBS News has gone to great lengths to insure that the public hears all sides of this complex situation. CBS News coverage of the energy crisis has, I believe, been fair and objective and has included significant opportunities for the presentation of the views of the oil industry. Between December and May, there were 45 individual appearances by oil industry spokesmen on CBS News television broadcasts. Two of these were interviews with Mobil's President and Mobil's Washington representative (both of whom expressed satisfaction at the way those interviews were handled). Mobil, in fact, rejected a CBS News proposal to feature the company on a *60 Minutes* report on the energy crisis. . . .

Certainly nobody, least of all broadcasters, maintains that journalists have done a perfect job on all occasions. But we believe that the way to insure that the public receives the full facts in an unbiased manner is not to turn the job over to the partisan of the issue with the most financial resources, but rather to see that all facts that the public needs are reported fairly and accurately on CBS News broadcasts.

This was the point that Chief Justice Burger was addressing when he rejected the notion that "every potential speaker is 'the best judge' of what the listening public ought to hear or indeed the best judge of the merits of his or her views. . . ." To the contrary, he wrote, "For better or worse, editing is what editors are for; and editing is selection and choice of material."

Far from restricting Mobil or the advocate of any other point of view, CBS will continue to present in the free forum of information those views that merit such coverage. That is the substance of independent journalism.

Just a few days after the above letter was sent, another aspect of the problems of the broadcaster in covering the news came into focus. For weeks, indeed months, broadcasters had been seeking to bring to the listening and viewing public all over the country the proceedings of the House Judiciary Committee's consideration of the question of impeaching the President. House rules had made it possible to keep the sessions off the air up to mid-July 1974.

CBS sent a telegram to the Speaker of the House and the Majority and Minority Leaders. Describing the public deliberations of the Judiciary Committee on the impeachment question, and any subsequent proceedings in the full House of Representatives, as "of transcendent political and historical importance to the people of the United States," we expressed our belief "that citizens have a right to as full and comprehensive an understanding of such proceedings as present-day communications technology makes possible." We said that opening the proceedings to live broadcast coverage "will firmly demonstrate the resolve of Congress to insure that the people have the right to participate as witnesses in these proceedings conducted by the people's own representatives." It was, we believe, a good thing for the country when the people, through television, received this first-hand view of the proceedings.

That is the essential function of broadcast news—to serve the people's right to know about the people's business, including the business of government. In broadcasting, of course, we are in the position of being licensed and regulated by government while we report on the activities of government. When we look back at the notable milestones of freedom for the broadcaster, as well as the notable challenges to that freedom, we find that too often the adversary is government.

Government, happily, is not the ultimate censor in our society. The ultimate determinant of what will be seen is the thumb and forefinger on the hand of the viewer or listener. If the audience turns the dial, the broadcast goes unheard, the television report unseen. But throughout the history of broadcasting, opponents of freedom have sought to use government for purposes of censorship, for purposes of mandating what broadcasters can say or do. Sadly, some advocates of freedom have mistakenly turned to government mandate, with exactly opposite results of what they sought.

Perhaps the best of all possible illustrations of this is Section 315 of the Communications Act, the so-called equal-time provision. It requires (with certain exceptions) that if time is given to one candidate for elective office all other candidates for the same office must be given equal time.

This sounds eminently fair, but its effect has been less than fair to the American public. It means, for example, that unless the law is changed — or, as only once, in 1960, suspended — broadcasting cannot give free time for face-to-face debates and other appearances of major party candidates without having to provide equal time for all the fringe candidates, numbering in some elections more than 20. The result, far from guaranteeing equal time to all candidates, is to bar time for any.

CBS has campaigned consistently for the repeal of Section 315. The print press has no such equal-time restriction. It has the editorial freedom to decide what space to devote to what candidates, and how to do it. Broadcasting seeks nothing more than this same freedom, on the basis of years of proven journalistic integrity.

If the people's rights are to be protected and the people's freedom upheld, it is vital that those with the responsibility of keeping the people informed are protected — not only as to the independence of their editorial and news judgments but also as to the integrity of their operations. Broadcast journalists cannot be treated as second-class citizens, barred from public governmental proceedings — Legislative or Judicial — to which their brethren of the print press are admitted. Journalists of all media must not be subjected to the chilling effect of subpoenas for their identification of confidential sources and notes and unpublished information — information central to the news-gathering process.

CBS management is not likely to forget that CBS is, after all, a business corporation. One of its principal purposes is to earn a profit, and with considerable regularity, it does so. But when I look at the newspapers I admire most in this country, I am struck by the fact that each of them operates with a similar philosophy — if the newspaper insists on highest standards of excellence, then the readers and the advertisers will follow almost as a matter of course. By and large, these newspapers have prospered.

At CBS, we have always tried to operate under the same principle, as a news medium, as an entertainment medium, and indeed in everything else we do. This setting down of a standard of excellence is in fact one of the heritages that William S. Paley has built into the Company. And we too have prospered.

At CBS, we make our decisions independently. This is never an easy task. Broadcasting's audience is all-inclusive, and many groups and people—political and otherwise—consider it imperative to keep subjects important to them off the air, or to get them on the air. And so we find ourselves constantly devoting vast portions of our working time simply to obtaining or preserving the freedom to fulfill our responsibilities.

One of the best means of creating informed public opinion as to the merits of various points of view, for example, is through the exchange of editorial opinions. Yet back in 1940, in the so-called Mayflower decision, the Federal Communications Commission said "The broadcaster cannot be an advocate" and thereby denied broadcasters the right to deliver editorials, however clearly these expressions of opinion might be labeled as expressions of opinion. In 1948, the FCC acceded to broadcasters' requests to reconsider the ban on editorials. CBS argued that freedom of expression and the right of advocacy were just as important for broadcasters as for any other journalistic media.

As a result of these hearings, the FCC reversed its previous decision and recognized the fundamental right of the broadcaster to editorialize, noting that the station must also play "a conscious and positive role in bringing about balanced presentation of the opposing viewpoint."

In the quarter of a century since this freedom was gained, CBS owned stations have led the way in bringing a variety of issues before the public through the presentation of editorials and editorial replies.

But other areas where freedom was still to be gained continued to pose problems. In the early 1950's CBS sought to have Section 315 repealed to make possible face-to-face discussions between the major Presidential candidates. The Network offered free time for such debates. The 1952 and 1956 elections went by with the equal-time ruling operating as a practical deterrent to free time for candidates, and in 1959 a partial victory was won when Public Law 86–274 was enacted, exempting various categories of news broadcasts from the equal-time rule. The following year, testifying before the Senate Subcommittee on Communications, CBS's Dr. Frank Stanton suggested a temporary suspension of Section 315 for the 1960 Presidential election. It was this temporary suspension which made possible the 1960 Kennedy–Nixon debates, but no permanent repeal of Section 315 ensued in the following three Presidential elections. There were offers of free network time from CBS and its affiliated stations in one election after another if the equal-time rule were suspended to make this possible. Congress, however, was also occupied with proposals for the compulsory allocation of air time, either purchased or simply assigned by governmental mandate, to candidates for federal office on the basis of one or another complicated formula.

CBS opposes the principle of mandated time on several counts, involving both considerations of freedom of the press and freedom of programming and also the sheer impracticality of the idea. In the New York metropolitan area, for example, where individual stations serve 40 Congressional districts in three states, such indiscriminate electioneering could consume, under one scheme, an estimated 106 of 123 primetime hours over the five-week period which, it was proposed, was to be set aside for such broadcasts in 1976. At the time these comments of mine are being written, the compulsory allocation of time for candidates' use has not passed the Congress and the public thankfully has been spared.

The problem of maintaining journalistic freedom for broadcasters goes far beyond the broadcasting of editorials or time for the advancement of ballot candidacies. In the recent past it has included (1) resisting efforts mounted by then Vice President Spiro Agnew in 1969, and taken up thereafter by other Nixon Administration figures, to increase licensees' awareness of the government's power, and whip up more support of Administration policies; (2) resisting the attempt to subpoena reporters' notes, unused film, and other confidential materials under threat of contempt of Congress citation, when the program "The Selling of the Pentagon" aroused the objections of some partisans; (3) facing contempt of court charges against reporters and other news people for refusing to reveal confidential sources and the like. CBS, a principal target both generally and as the broadcaster of "The Selling of the Pentagon," has steadfastly fought to defend basic journalistic freedom in these matters. The contempt of Congress citation was defeated in the House of Representatives; CBS has supported proposals for newsmen's shield legislation which would be applicable to both federal and state proceedings.

Significantly, the various challenges to journalistic freedom of the broadcaster that I have mentioned have come from different branches of the government—Executive, Legislative, and Judicial. We believe that the vigor and promptness of our response has been important in causing wiser counsels ultimately to prevail. And we also realize that the battles are never-ending.

Judges, grand juries, and other local, state, and federal officials are still sometimes inclined to attempt to make the news media an investigative arm of the government. All too recently, newsmen have gone to jail for refusing to hand over unpublished information to courts or to grand juries. Attempts have been made all too recently to deny television license renewals to stations owned by newspapers, even after it has been demonstrated in Boston that the loss of broadcast revenues can silence a newspaper. (The loss of the WHDH–TV license in Boston led to the collapse of the *Herald-Traveler*.)

It is our strong feeling that the public is ill served by arbitrary and capricious use of government power, however well intended. Taken individually, many steps to limit the freedom of operation of broadcast or print journalism may not seem major in their impact. But in sum, the cumulative effect could be to cripple our ability to provide information vital to the citizens of a democracy.

Many of the proposals for government action have been based on assertions that news as a process is "controlled" by three networks or two or three major newspapers, and that there is need for more diversity. We strongly reject such assertions.

In 1974, when Americans were spending, in an average week, 555 million hours watching television news broadcasts, 394 million of these hours were spent on locally produced news and 161 million hours on network news broadcasts. In radio the overwhelming proportion of news is locally produced.

But while we assuredly need the local media, we also need media with the resources to operate on a transcontinental and worldwide scale. For it is only such big, well-financed media that can, with adequacy, cover our big, well-financed government; that can serve our transcontinental society; that can deal meaningfully with ideas, concepts, and events that are worldwide.

Much of the financial support for broadcast journalism comes from the revenues of entertainment programming, and what limits the freedom of one branch of the media—broadcast or print—represents a danger to the freedom of all. I remember Eric Sevareid's remark when he warned newspapermen that to ignore government threats against broadcasters because print is not immediately threatened is like saying "Your end of the boat is sinking."

It is a tragedy if either end of the boat should begin to sink. But sometimes the principal danger is that we don't keep ourselves alert enough to how important it is to keep afloat. This is not a matter of business investment; it is a matter of the public interest. Lack of proper communication of news and information is, without exaggeration, a matter of life and death. Let's go back into history for a tangible example.

The Battle of New Orleans a century and a half ago was fought after the war ended. In 1815, 2,000 men marched off to die without knowing that, 15 days earlier, a peace treaty had been signed in Europe to end the fighting. That needlessly tragic conclusion to the War of 1812 was in keeping with the war's beginning. The first shots were fired two days after Great Britain agreed to repeal the laws over which that nation and our own were to go to war.

Better communications might have made the beginning and ending to that conflict happier. But it was not until the advent of the telegraph, in the 1840's, that communications left the horse trails and took to the air. This was a considerable aid to governments and their military commanders, but to the average American citizen, by the time news was printed and distributed, it no longer seemed a current event to which he might react. And if domestic news read like history, news of foreign developments must have taken on overtones of ancient history. The wireless in the 1890's was a further improvement, but only with the development of radio in the twentieth century did world events for the first time become immediate and significant to the American public, rather than remote and relatively unimportant.

Motion pictures, including newsreels, added realism to reporting, but they lacked immediacy and were usually seen days and even weeks after the event. It was not until the Vietnam war, for the first time in history, that millions of people here and abroad could virtually be present at battles being fought halfway around the world. They witnessed, in living color and sound, daily developments on the battlefields of Vietnam and in the streets of Saigon. Anyone with access to a television set became, at the flick of a switch, able to see what was transpiring in remote villages, the names of which most of us had never heard and, at least initially, could not even pronounce. Furthermore, the television viewer here and abroad could hear from their own lips within hours what the men and women on the scene in Vietnam were saying and thinking and doing.

With the addition of television to the many other tools the press corps employs, Vietnam was the best reported war in history. It was also a major domestic issue, in which the role of journalism itself became an issue. But out of that war and out of Watergate has come further proof of the wisdom of James Madison's often quoted advice that "A people who mean to be their own governors must arm themselves with the power that knowledge gives. A popular government without popular information, or the means of acquiring it, is but a prologue to a farce or a tragedy."

On the occasion of the dedication of the second unit of the Newhouse Communications Center at Syracuse University in the spring of 1974, CBS Chairman William S. Paley recalled and renewed an expression that sums up why broadcasting fights to maintain its journalistic freedom. Said Mr. Paley:

Twenty years ago—almost to the day—I had occasion to address myself to the freedom and responsibility of broadcasters. I said then, "Some people may question the desirability of placing in the hands of the broadcaster this important element of control. To this point I would say that undoubtedly there may be abuses, as there are in other media. But I for one have enough faith in the vitality of the democratic process, in the intelligence of the American people, and in the freshness of the competitive climate to believe that the good will and the determined intent of broadcasters to be fair, coupled with the powerful voice of the people, will provide far better protection against abuse than any other form of control."

Nothing during the past 20 years has led me to change my mind or to qualify those words.

If there is any risk—and there is—in this belief that, to quote Jefferson's words,'. . . the people . . . may safely be trusted to hear everything true and false, and to form a correct judgment between them'—and there is a risk— then it is the risk basic and continuous in any free society. But it has been the verdict of our forebears and the experience of ourselves that a free society is not the safest way of life: it is only the best.

CHARLES EVERS

In the early 1950's Charles and Medgar Evers quietly began to organize NAACP memberships and branches throughout Mississippi.

After his brother was murdered by hidden assailants on June 12, 1963, Charles Evers assumed Medgar's responsibilities as State Field Secretary of the Mississippi NAACP.

Voter registration of blacks, which was linked to the assassination of Medgar, was expanded across Mississippi by Charles Evers. Black voter registration increased from 28,500 in 1965 to 250,000 in 1972.

For the first time in modern history a Negro—Charles Evers—ran for the office of U.S. Representative in Mississippi. In 1968, Evers won the primary with a plurality. In the runoff he lost to a white candidate.

The following year Charles Evers was elected Mayor of Fayette, Mississippi, the first black mayor of a biracial town in Mississippi's history. Fayette is located in Jefferson County, which in 1969 was the fourth poorest in America.

Within weeks, Mayor Evers launched a series of programs to attract resources and personnel that began to transform Fayette and Jefferson County from one of the poorest to one of the most promising in the rural South. Today Fayette boasts a panoply of social services and economic self-help programs that have produced jobs, better health, higher living levels, sensitive police administration, and good government. All of these had been in exceedingly short supply in most of Mississippi.

In 1971, Charles Evers waged a dynamic campaign for Governor of the State of Mississippi, the first black candidate since Reconstruction. This unprecedented effort attracted volunteers from every section of the nation, including blacks and whites, young and old, rich and poor. Among the national figures who campaigned for the Evers candidacy and those of 136 blacks running for local office were Mrs. Martin Luther King, Jr., Mayor John V. Lindsay, Mayor Richard Hatcher, Congressmen Louis Stokes, Charles Diggs, John Conyers, Parren Mitchell, Rev. Robert F. Drinan, and former JFK aide Theodore C. Sorensen. Despite harassment, threats and intimidation, almost one fourth of the voters cast their ballots for Charles Evers, and 51 blacks were elected to local office, giving Mississippi a total of 118 elected black officials, third highest in the nation.

Chapter **9**

The Fayette Experiment

Edited from discussions and tapes with
CHARLES EVERS

Fayette, Mississippi was a played out cotton town back in 1969, impoverished, a backwater of hate and bigotry that deeply split its 1,100 black and 500 white residents. Its future was as bleak as the thousands of other sleepy little Southern towns whose industry was nonexistent, whose economy was stagnated, whose people lived in fear and distrust of their neighbors.

And then on May 13, 1969, Charles Evers, brother of slain civil rights leader Medgar Evers, was elected mayor, the first black in Mississippi history to win such a post in a biracial town. Swept into office with him was the entire slate of five Negro aldermen, starting what was to be known as "The Fayette Experiment."

In this one tiny leap Evers became the embodiment and projection of all the South's best hopes for the future. It was a time of political change in the nation and weathered campaign signs from the past proclaimed, "Let us all go forward together." And with Evers' election he proclaimed, "No more hate, no more guns. Blacks and whites, rich and poor, are going to live and work and die in Fayette."

Before Evers' election there had been a decade of hard, dangerous and patient work in which the black citizens of Mississippi used the ballot box to overcome local racist rule. During the prolonged struggle, many Negroes lost their lives, as did white sympathizers who came down from the North to help.

Medgar Evers, Field Secretary of the National Association for the Advancement of Colored People (NAACP) was slain in cold blood in 1963 because of his courageous and stubborn efforts to register Negro voters. Charles Evers succeeded him in the post of Field Secretary and even today is harassed by white die-hards.

Charles Evers had many friends in the battle for racial equality,

131

including Dr. Martin Luther King, Jr. And like him, Evers also had a dream—one he lived to see come true. It was a broad program that included civic programs for blacks and whites, an industrialization program that would lift Fayette and surrounding Jefferson County from a condition in which 65 per cent of the people received $30 a month in welfare funds. Jefferson County was the fourth poorest county in the nation.

It was a big dream for such a time and place, yet in the next few years Evers was to achieve his goals, one of the first of which was to furnish 500 new jobs to end the dependence on welfare and to bring Jefferson County to a level approaching the national median. Grants from a special fund had made possible the growth of city and county services, which created some employment. Evers' goal of 500 jobs became possible in March, 1970, when International Telephone and Telegraph agreed to establish a $174,000 plant, the first occupant of the 250-acre industrial park corporation Evers had carved from the Mississippi mud, a plant that was to give Fayette a monthly payroll of $40,000.

Evers, who had searched the land for industry, summed it up: "No one heard us but ITT."

Evers began putting the Fayette Experiment into effect the moment he took office. His first public act as mayor was to bar all forms of racial discrimination in public accommodations and facilities—a furtherance of his civil rights campaign of the past years in which he had braved death many times to knock down the barriers of segregation.

His victory celebration on inaugural day took place in the Confederate Square at the town's center, a small park that had been barred to blacks since it had come into being. It was a symbolic act, but it marked the beginning of the experiment. It indicated to all concerned that Fayette would no longer tolerate the institutional racism upon which the historic social and economic system of the South had previously been based. The symbolic event was followed by a series of new ordinances designed to remove all racial bars from the lives of the overwhelming black majority in Fayette.

There came a series of public works programs to give employment to black and white, for always in Evers' mind were the almost staggering economic facts. Jefferson County had been declining since the turn of the century. The median income of white families was $4,280, that of blacks $890. The per capita income came to about $1,000, and unemployment was indeed overwhelming.

Tough new ordinances forced school attendance. There were ordinances to ensure equal treatment for the minority whites. With the advent of public work programs, Fayette's economy began a slow climb upward, and with it the cooperation of the white merchants — the power of green was proving to be more compelling than racial interests.

Evers' attempts to improve the economic situation were likened to a bootstrap operation — without the boots. He commissioned an economic survey which showed that Fayette needed 500 jobs just to raise the income to a national median, 800 jobs if it were to have a viable tax base to keep his administration running.

But before there could be industry there had to be improvement in the town of Fayette and in Jefferson County. From grants, Fayette began rebuilding and expanding its infrastructure with health and social services, roads, streets, and sewage and water plants, law enforcement agencies, an industrial park, training services, and other facilities which simply did not exist.

There was help from unexpected quarters. The Philadelphia Black Policemen's Association donated a police car, and Evers was able to buy a large garbage truck from New York City for $1. Philadelphia also sent a skilled black police officer, Alphonso Deal, to train the small Fayette police force. There were other donations — an ambulance, an accounting machine, funds for a swimming pool. At one point, 100 Michigan doctors, working in shifts, helped to organize health facilities.

The Fayette Experiment began working, but transforming paper recommendations into concrete achievements required a flow of capital, similar in some ways to the Marshall Plan, which came into being to aid postwar Europe. While his associates worked at home, Evers worked to attract industry. It is estimated that in the first 1,500 days of his administration he held 700 to 800 meetings with potential investors and flew more than 200,000 miles.

This appeal to industry was made on radio and television throughout the nation. As Evers remembers, "We sent out all kinds of letters to different organizations and whenever there was a meeting of industrialists, I would go there and make a personal appeal to them. ITT was the only one that heard us . . . it was just that simple, and they came."

There already had been dramatic improvements in Fayette. Through his public works and other programs financed through the Medgar Evers Fund, unemployment dropped from 65 per cent in the spring of 1969 to 29 per cent in March, 1974. The average income of black families rose from $890 a year to between $4,400 and $6,000. The need was still for industry.

Through his own efforts, Evers inaugurated enough projects to employ 350 persons, but he was far short of his goal. That was when ITT stepped into the picture, largely through the influence of Senator Edward M. Kennedy, who personally pleaded Evers' case.

It was in March, 1970, that the ITT Thompson Industries announced it would build a plant in Fayette to manufacture circuit controls and automotive wire harnesses with anti-pollution devices for Ford and Chrysler cars. The wire harness assemblies are the complicated wiring that connects sparkplugs to the distributor—a complex, precision product.

ITT made a study of the area and the availability of labor for a plant. The picture was not bright, but it was decided to open a training program to see if the farm or unemployed people could learn to make the automobile parts.

Two local white businessmen agreed to finance and build the plant and lease it to ITT. They were Carrol G. McLaurin, a Chevrolet dealer, and Charles N. Montgomery, Jr., the owner of a local supermarket. Their faith in Evers' industrialization program was more evidence of Evers' progress in winning the respect of the white community.

With construction of the plant under way, the vocational training program picked up momentum. ITT furnished know-how and necessary equipment. When they were ready to hire for the ITT plant, there was a small core of trained workers ready to begin work.

Fayette is a backwater, of course, but it feels the impact of national economics—the 1970 recession, for example, soon made itself felt in Fayette and slowed Evers' program to bring in more industry.

There were a few garment and textile industries interested in Fayette, but when the recession came, these industries decided they couldn't move or expand at that time. Evers says:

> In the meantime ITT Thompson has had a big impact in Fayette. The payroll for this plant is over $40,000. The payroll alone means a great deal to a community that had nothing.
>
> It helped everybody—it affected the whole community. Since then we have a new shopping center, the Fayette Plaza. That came because of the industry of ITT and the money that they pay out. We have a new furniture store because of this. You see people come to a town that is growing and booming and that's why we hope that ITT will stay with us because we can't afford not to have them.
>
> I remember the opening. We had a ground breaking ceremony and then we had a grand opening ceremony. Arthur T. Woerthwein, ITT Group Vice President, was present at the opening.
>
> It took a combination to get that plant here. It was kind of a three-way deal—the Fayette government, local money, and ITT.
>
> Senator Kennedy was also very helpful. His calls to ITT got us together and I took over from there.
>
> Industry had let us down in the olden days because they played their role with a big stick, and money is the big stick. Now we are not going to have that. If you are black or white you are not going to get a job here if you are not going to work together. You see industry has helped to provoke and project racism by putting white signs and black signs and Negro signs and all that crap around and having only demeaning jobs for blacks. Well, ITT

hasn't done that here. Our top supervisor is as black as I am. His name is Dave Berry.

Berry, a salaried foreman, is 30. He works as the foreman during the day in the moulding and pressing departments, and during the night shift there is another young black foreman named Ernest Green, 32.

There were 144 people working in the plant in early 1974, including operators in the plant's cutting department, press department, moulding department, final assembly, hand taping, welding, and soldering. There are also material handlers in shipping and receiving and quality assurance. The total work force is 85 per cent black, and two of the three girls working in the office are black.

Corrie Lee Hunt, Delores Day, and Mattie Collier have risen from the ranks to semi-supervisory status at the plant. They are officially called lead operators and their job is to keep the heart of the plant — the rotary — supplied with material. The rotary is a machine with movable stations and amounts to a stationary assembly line with the stations moving around the machine. Use of the rotary permits four to six workers, each with a specific job, to work close together instead of being strung out along an assembly line.

"Dave was the first one to receive training and he came up through the ranks and now he is supervisor," Evers said. "This is all we wanted. We just wanted someone to give us a chance. And if we can't do it, all right, but not just because you're black or because you're white. . . .

"With ITT here we've had a little expansion. We also got a little concrete and mixing plant, small, but it is five or six people. We got the shopping center which employs about 20 people and we got blacks owning service stations and this kind of thing and this employs about 10 people. So I don't mean that ITT is the *only* business, but it shows what happens when a major industry comes in."

The first group of persons seeking work at ITT Thompson began their training on simple assembly line machinery. Some, not accustomed to working in team fashion, were unable to grasp the techniques. Others took to it naturally, and they became the nucleus of a labor force for the plant.

As the techniques improved, so did the quality of the products, and the more skillful workers assisted the newcomers under the guidance of an ITT manager and the foreman.

Gradually the roles increased and the work was expanded into two shifts employing 160 persons, who poured a large payroll into the town of Fayette and aided the prosperity of others.

The contracts for the harnesses increased and two major car manufacturers began buying the vital equipment. A tight quality control program reduced failures to a tiny percentage. A close watch is maintained, with testing, over each batch of wiring.

Instead of trying to subsist on welfare checks of barely $30 a month, the workers now receive around $100 a week.

"No one can ever run down a corporation like ITT to me," Evers said. "ITT has saved my community. It has taken all of these people off welfare and given them a personal pride in a job well done. In a poverty area such as this, ITT has come in and done a real job. I'll forever be grateful for their helping our citizens."

But the plant, begun as a social experiment, was faced immediately with crisis—a devastating automobile strike that kept the tiny plant struggling for survival, with the payroll at times as small as 15 persons. However, the strike ended and by December, 1972, the plant was employing its full capacity of 160 persons, with a backlog of orders and the highest efficiency rating among its fellow plants in the South.

The assembly line workers included a healthy sprinkling of local whites, who, like their black colleagues, had been on welfare for the past few years. Now they too were making $100 a week instead of receiving the $30 monthly welfare.

MEDGAR EVERS FUND

If it was ITT Thompson Industries which gave Evers the first big break in bringing industry to Fayette, it was the Medgar Evers Fund which started the Fayette Experiment moving toward success and eventual industrialization.

The fund was founded in September, 1969, both to perpetuate the memory of the martyred civil rights leader and to support programs of social and economic advancement in the Fayette region. Two dozen prominent Americans, both black and white, joined to form the non-profit organization.

The most active were—in addition to Mayor Evers and Mrs. Myrlie Evers, Medgar's widow—Ted Sorensen, John Doar, Mrs. Edward M. Warburg, Mrs. Anne Rockefeller Coste, Father William Morrissey, George Backer, Judge Robert L. Carter, Joe Rauh, Stanley Kaplan, Dr. Aaron Henry, and Judge William Booth.

By early 1972 more than 30,000 Americans had contributed to Fayette's development through the fund, and more than $680,000 was pumped into Fayette. This helped the town to generate millions of dollars in public funding, which radically altered the local infrastructure and which helped to achieve the new administration's first priority—new jobs. Evers puts the figure at $10 million from federal and private sources.

Much of the fund's grants to Fayette have enabled the town to come forth with local share-matching grants toward federal grants of much greater amounts. Among the projects funded were a five-year, $5 million two-county comprehensive health program now treating 8,000 persons in Jefferson and neighboring Claiborne County, a multipurpose community center, a child day care center, an economic development office, a dental program, a training program for municipal employees, a project to train and equip the local police force, a recreation program which included construction of a swimming pool and two modern playgrounds, plus scholarships.

But the need in Fayette was industry and for that Evers turned to big business.

We are still sending out the letters, but so far we haven't been able to get anyone, and that's why I say that when people attack ITT they haven't looked at all the good ITT has done, particularly in communities where people really need it. It is the working man that is hurt when big business does not help.

We hoped that someone would come to Fayette. We needed jobs. We had plenty of labor. We sent all over the country to everybody and we went to everybody and finally somebody said, "Why don't you try ITT?" And I said, "Hell, ITT wouldn't come to a place like this, why should they come?" And they said "Try them." And then I called my friend, Senator Kennedy—Ted Kennedy—and a couple of my friends and they contacted them and they set up a meeting for us and from that we got the plant.

I was shocked, they showed some concern. In fact they showed more than concern, they were interested right off the bat. And they said, "We are going to see what we can do," and I thought that would be the end of it. And in about three weeks we heard from one person and then from another person and they finally came down here and some of the executives came down and looked over what we had, and they sent back word of what the company would need. And then we got busy and got the plant, got it financed through private sources here. . . .

Without big business in this country we don't make it, we would be another India, another Africa, where there is nothing going on but poverty and hunger and bad living. . . . All I can say is that in Fayette ITT came when we needed them. Sixty-five per cent of our people were on welfare when they came here. Yes, 65 per cent were on welfare, were unemployed, and now we're down to about 29 per cent [March, 1974]. ITT didn't do it all but it did one hell of a slug on it. . . . Of the people who started at the ITT plant, 90 per cent were on welfare, getting $30 a month. Now we have 60 people making around $75 to $100 a week. So you see that's a hell of a long ways and they got good housing now, and most of them have bought some decent furniture and they have bought a decent car and they walk the streets and they can feel like they are somebody. . . .

Another thing about big business, transforming Fayette or similar communities is the most important thing industry can do and I would even advise industry not to cluster in one place but go throughout the nation in small communities. This helps in two areas. First, it helps keep people at home. They don't go somewhere to find a job and get there and become unemployed and disgusted and become criminals.

It also provides light in a community, and there wouldn't be light if it weren't for the industry. That's why I feel that it's so important for industry to go to the small places and provide a service, provide an income, provide a life for these people. Most of the people who get in trouble in New York and Chicago are our ex-Southern boys and girls and men and women. They—particularly in Chicago, most people in Chicago came from Mississippi and Tennessee—leave here going to Chicago to get a job, and when they get to Chicago, they can't get a job. So they get on welfare. They start stealing their stuff, robbing and all of those things and then they get in trouble. If industry had provided a job for them back home maybe they wouldn't have left home in the first place. If we just look at it from what it really means, and the value of it, you find that it means so much to a community if it can just get more industry. And ITT, I think, has done one heck of a job in a lot of places.

The way we got involved goes all the way back to the first meeting set up by Senator Ted Kennedy, through his office in New York and in Washington, and some people from ITT. They were very receptive. They sat there and listened and when we got through telling them the story and got to talking with them, they were very concerned. Some delegates from ITT flew down here and I showed them what I was talking about. Then they went back and went through the protocol, or whatever it takes to get a plant located. Then they came back for another look and to inquire how we would build the facilities.

We knew how to build it. We didn't know where we would get the money, because we didn't have any money. We just had faith that if they would come we would get a building. Then I let some of my white friends know that we could get a plant if we could get a building. And right away, these two local men, the Chevrolet dealer and the supermarket man, came and said they would build the building.

And I said, "You're kidding," and they said, "No, we're not." We have an industrial park and we let them have the land for $200. They built the building and they said that if we could get a commitment from ITT that they would rent it to ITT for a period of 10 or 15 years.

You'd be surprised what a short time it took from the first time the ITT people came to Fayette. It was so short that it frightened me—it must have been not over four months. . . . And it was only about a year before the plant was in operation. It opened up and we started off with I think 10 people, maybe 15. Even before the plant opened there was a lot of reaction in the community that an industrial plant was coming.

We set up—we have a vocational school—and we set up in there a training school, a training course preparing them for the division that was coming, and we had—we must have had 500 people standing in line to get in there. You could just see it on their faces that we were getting a plant and that we were going to have jobs and we were going to have this. And that's what I try to tell white people in this country—that 99 per cent of black folks are on welfare because they've got no choice. If they had a choice there would be a chance and a job.

I don't think that ITT can say that they have had trouble out of the employees. We have a little squabble once in a while but as far as trouble is concerned, all we ask ITT is to be fair with us and give them a fair shake.

The interesting thing is the white reaction to the plant. First, there were two whites who built the plant. Then there were whites lining up for jobs. I don't know how many we had, but we must have had 10 or 15 whites out there. That may not sound like a lot, but it is a hell of a lot of white people for a town, for a community that has been predominantly black and that has been one of the worst racist, Ku Klux Klan areas in the country. And now you find black and white men and women working side by side in the programs and in the ITT plant and it's because of economics. That's what I keep saying all the time — most of our problems are economic. When you bring the money in, you tell somebody that you get a dollar if you work side by side with that black boy. You say, "Hell no," and I say, "You don't get the dollar." Then after a while they will say, "The hell with it, I'll go with a black boy, a blue boy, or a colored boy, it doesn't matter to me, but I'm going to get paid a dollar," and that's what it's all about.

And that's why an outfit like ITT can be so helpful in this country and help end racism and discrimination in this country in politics by just standing up for what is right. And that is what ITT has done here, and I don't care what they did in San Francisco or what happened in South America. That doesn't mean a damn thing to me but what they did for my folks here, that's what counts. Here is a living example. Look how the folks live and now they have good housing and look at the clothes they wear. They used to wear old raggedy clothes and old rundown shoes. No more of that mess. And that's what it has meant to us. It has meant a lot. It has meant life to us. It has meant an independent feeling.

Another thing, you can't really separate the social aspects from the economic aspects. They're both together. The lower economic group has been brought together and the problem of this country is that blacks and whites don't know each other. We live in two different worlds. And it is because one group feels superior to the other and when you really boil it down, what we have done here along with ITT, we proved that we're all just folks. It doesn't matter a damn what color you are. If you're hungry, you're hungry. If you're poor, you're poor. If you're on the welfare, you're on the welfare.

It doesn't matter if you're black or white, and if you can get a job paying $2 an hour and that's going to help you eat better, sleep better, live better. . . . black or white. And this is the kind of thing that this industry has done here. It has brought poor whites who used to run around with sheets on their damn heads at night killing black people. Now they're working side by side. Go and see. They work side by side right at the plant. Now they are friends and that's "Ole John" and that's "Ole Charles" and that's "Ole Sally" and that's "Ole Helen" and that's just the way it is, but it took that money to bring it about. You [whites] must be crazy if you are going to sit by and let us have all of these good jobs. You mean you're going to let your white pride stop you from eating good, stop your child from going to a decent school, or stop you from having a decent car? Your answer should be no.

People ask me how we got started. Well, we built better schools, better libraries, paved streets, and the first real garbage collection. And this was before there was industry to pay taxes. I think you first have to show you have to have ability, and then you must show leadership. You see it's who sits at the top who will determine how a community goes.

If you're a bunch of lazy do-nothing folks who sit around and talk — well — but if you have an aggressive administration, then the people will follow. If we had just been complacent, then we would die waiting. If you don't holler and scream for help and try to show what you need, then you won't get anything. Every town ought to do what I've done, or what I've tried to do. They have got to go out and go to ITT, General Motors, whoever they are and tell them. We told ITT what we wanted and they responded.

Before a town can ask industry to come in, it must make itself suitable and attractive. You must have good police protection and law and order. If you break the law you pay for it.

I loved the Kennedys and I had great respect for President Johnson. When he asked for the Voting Rights Bill, he told Congress, "The Negro citizen may go to register only to be told that the day is wrong, or the hour is late, or the official in charge is absent." Johnson is a favorite of mine. I'm against war 101 per cent, and I've been against all wars. I'm not going to let Johnson's domestic programs be overshadowed by his stand on Vietnam. I'm proud that he cared enough and was big enough to carry out John Kennedy's program. I don't think you can say that about very many other presidents. President Johnson carried it out almost to the letter.

It was President Johnson who put the Civil Rights bill through, who made it possible for us to eat in the hotels and motels and to get a drink of water out of any fountain.

My honeymoon with Washington ended in 1969 when I became mayor of Fayette and a new administration took over. As the first year of the Nixon Administration progressed, it appeared increasingly unsympathetic to the aspirations of blacks and other minorities. It forged its New Majority with a Southern Strategy designed to appeal exclusively to the region's whites. And by the end of the year, the first effects of a prolonged recession began to be felt as well. By 1970 major corporations were closing down plants across the South, instead of considering new sites for expansion. People began feeling the economic pinch and contributions and grants began to dwindle. By the next year the backlash among white moderates was itself a facet of considerable importance.

I don't fight Nixon. Hell, no. I don't fight Nixon. I'm part of the government too, and my job is to provide. If I go and cuss Nixon, do you think I'm going to get water and sewage plants and get interest from ITT? Hell, no. If you don't have water and sewers, there is no reason for ITT or any other company to come here. You've got to have something to offer. The town has got to have something to offer. You have to have an administration, a vigorous, aggressive administration. You can't have racist strife. We don't allow black or white organizing in this town. If somebody calls a white person "honkie" in this town it will cost them $100. If somebody calls a black "nigger" in this town, it will cost them $100. We just don't allow it. We fine them for disturbing the "nigger's" peace, or for disturbing the "honkie's" peace. If somebody calls you a "honkie," that's an insult to you and you disturb his peace, and the statutes say anytime a person disturbs another person's personal peace you can fine him for it. So we fine them. We just don't intend to keep on having racial strife.

And you don't see anybody with guns. When industry comes in they look at that and they say, "Hey, what's the atmosphere here? What's the attitude?" And if you come in and get a tense feeling you aren't going to spend a million dollars in a place where there is all that tension.

NEED FOR ACTION

Action has to be taken. And action seems to win the people—my whole thing about democracy is that the people are the democracy, that when they go to vote for you to be the mayor or the president, then they give you the authority to do what you think is best for them. That's why they voted you in there, and if you don't do what is best for them, let them replace you and put somebody else in there—but you can't have everybody running the council meeting. You just can't do that. You never get it done if you have a 100 people. You have a 100 different ideas. All night long you could argue about what time we should go to school. So you are going to build a school big enough to open from 8 in the morning till 3 in the afternoon. You got to say that, and then do it, because if you don't you can't get anything done.

People sometimes ask if we need an Industrial Board or a Chamber of Commerce to seek industry. Well, I have those, but we don't depend on them to bring in business.

My whole thing is, you do it. You just do it. My job is to get some industry, and some help. So if people ask about an Industrial Board I say, "No, I have a group of people around me, and of course I have people all over the country who serve as a committee to help me. I have people in New York. I have them in Florida, Chicago, and California. And then I have my own employees here. We all work to bring in industry. The idea is to produce. You can't just sit around and say, "I'm Charles Evers, the mayor," and not do a damn thing.

EVERS—THE MAN

To understand Evers the mayor one must understand Evers the man and his incredible rise in Mississippi politics. A little more than a decade ago a Negro in Mississippi was often thought of as no better than a mule by white racists—a subhuman creature, a beast of burden with slightly more intelligence than the four-legged variety. It was a life of bullying by white children, of constant hatred, of petty tyrannies, and of farmers who hired Negro children to pick pecans or grind sugar cane. Black boys stepped off the sidewalk when a white woman passed, for an accidental brushing could end in lynching. There was one notable case of a youth being lynched because he "looked the wrong way" at a white woman.

It was a period when Evers' mother, who wanted everything for her children, worked as cook and laundress and maid for the white folks at $2.50 a week. It was a period when schooling for blacks lasted only four months a year because Negro children were taken out of school to till the fields.

The question, "When did you know you were black?" is unfair. There is no black man in this country who'll tell the truth, who won't say he has known he has been black all his life. He has been mistreated like he's inhuman. . . . Being black is part of the air you breathe. Our mothers began telling us about being black from the day we were born. The white folks weren't any better than we were, Momma said, but they sure thought they were. When we'd ask why we couldn't do something or the other, often she'd just say, "Because you're colored, son."

Medgar and I, right from the start, when we were little kids, were determined to prove that this wasn't a white man's world—or if it was, we'd at least get our share of whatever there was worth getting and see that some other black folks could, too.

My Momma was strong and my Daddy was strong, and they influenced my life the most. I got my religion from my Momma and my Daddy taught me not to be afraid.

Daddy was a mean man. He couldn't read or write, but he didn't back off of any man, white or black. His name was Jim Evers. He was tall, over six feet, like me. He didn't have the kind of trouble that many blacks had, because Daddy was so mean. He worked hard but he wasn't a bit scary. He taught me that most white folks are cowards. If they haven't got you outnumbered, you can back 'em down. So I've always thought I could outfight most white folks. Being black, you gotta learn that, just to survive. . . .

White folks used to call him a "crazy nigger" 'cause they couldn't scare him or make him crawl. He worked hard, from sunup to sundown, but he never let white folks break his spirit. Looking back I don't know how he ever survived back in the '20's and '30's when the Klan was riding high and things were bad.

I remember on Christmas Eve the white folks would always celebrate by shooting off fireworks, Roman candles and sparklers and firecrackers. And Medgar and me, we felt bad cause we weren't allowed to see it. No colored folks was allowed in town by the Klan. But our Daddy, he saw how we felt and he told us, "C'mon boys, we going to town." And he took a baseball bat he'd made for us out of an old broom handle, and he said, "If anybody throws a firecracker at us, we gonna use this on him."

So we walked down the road to Decatur and the white folks along the way just stood there staring at us, their mouths hanging open. Once a white kid ran up in front of us and he was about to light a firecracker, so my Daddy said, "You throw that firecracker and I'll bust your brains out." He ran and told his father, who came up all mad looking, but my Daddy just told him, "That goes for you, too." The white man backed right down and nobody gave us any trouble. That night we thought the Klan might come out to get us, so we sat up all Christmas Eve with rifles, waiting for 'em, but nobody came. . . . It was lucky for them they didn't. We'd have killed every one of 'em. Medgar and me, we were really disappointed they didn't come.

I was about ten and Medgar about eight when local whites in Decatur killed one of our father's friends, Willie Tingle. Mr. Tingle was supposed to have looked at a white woman, or insulted her. They dragged him through the street behind a wagon and hung him up to a tree and shot at him. Later, when I was a grown man I'd go back to Decatur and see these same white folks who killed Mr. Tingle. One of them was drying up like a seed, I thought: "He must remember the night he and the other hate-mongers killed Mr. Tingle."

The way they treated him really got Medgar and me bitter toward white people. . . . We knew we had to do something about it. . . .

Sometimes it was just no fun growing up black, like when we got it hammered into us to watch our step, to stay in our place, or get off the street when a white woman passed by so as not to brush up against her accidentally. To be black in this country is miserable more often than it's not.

As the brothers grew older they changed. Medgar became more saintly, more gentle. Charles became less saintly, more interested in money.

"Sometimes when people would say I was living high on the hog I'd say, 'Well, you go to hell. I worked 15 to 16 hours a day to get what I got. Sure I want to make money. That's why I'm in business, to make money. I don't see nothin' wrong with making money.' You can't do anything broke. If black people are to be really free in Mississippi, or any place else, we need to own something."

Evers became a successful businessman in the early 1960's but was bankrupted by white pressure. He went to Chicago and he made money by every means he could—he was involved in prostitution, in the policy racket, and he ended up with an apartment house and a popular bar.

"I want people to know I've never been a saint," Evers said. "Can't nobody tell on me more than I've already told. . . . I'm still going to be a man." And when he ran unsuccessfully as Democratic candidate for governor of Mississippi in 1971 he frankly admitted his lurid past with the explanation he would rather bring it out into the open than have his political opponents use it as campaign material.

"Racism drove me to it—no jobs or anything," he said. "I'm in politics now. I don't want anybody to support me and not know what I have been."

Evers' first brush with bootlegging came in his youth. His family owned funeral parlors at Philadelphia, Forest, and Mount Olive, Mississippi, and bootlegging was widespread in a state that remained dry until 1966.

Uncle Mark had an ambulance and a hearse. And whenever I learned that he was away I'd get in the ambulance and go to Vicksburg where they sold sealed whiskey. I was too young to buy, but I paid off an older man to buy it and carry it to his garage. I'd take Medgar or somebody with me in the ambulance and when I'd get the whiskey I'd hide it under the ambulance bed and make whoever was with me get in the bed and lie down and I'd return with the siren open. I'd come through all those small towns with the sirens blasting. Screaming sirens and bootleg whiskey. I'd just be rolling and people would be getting out of the way. I'd carry the whiskey into Forest about dark, drive up into the shed where we kept the ambulance, pull the door down and run in and get the "dead man cot" and unload my whiskey on it and carry it into the embalming room. I'd take the embalming fluid aside and start stacking my whiskey and put the fluid on top of the whiskey.

This way I kept my sealed whiskey, scotch, bourbon, and gin. I had men who'd sell it for me. If someone wanted 50 half-pints, I'd give them 50 half-pints, and they would sell it and bring the money back. No one could say that I was selling whiskey. I was the one backing all the bootleggers.

Evers served in Australia, New Guinea, and the Philippines in an all black combat engineers outfit during a 1946–1951 stint in the U.S. Army.

Evers returned to Mississippi after the war and enrolled in Alcorn A & M College in Lorman, Mississippi, where he majored in social science and played football. He worked as a disc jockey and established various small business enterprises in Philadelphia, Mississippi, after serving another hitch in the army during the Korean War. He and Medgar began a NAACP membership drive in 1951 and it was then when Charles was forced to go to Chicago to acquire sufficient capital to continue.

Man, it was rough in Chicago. We bought day-old bread and neck bones, 50 cents' worth at a time. We lived in a basement with the roaches, water dripping through the pipes. We'd go to bed and the rats were with us. . . .

Somehow the Lord took care of me. I just kept going for three long years. I didn't do anything but work and go to church on Sunday.

I turned to policy. I started out as a runner. I was dropping policy, picking up policy—a field runner. As I learned the game I began to drop my own policy, on the same route, under the same protection. I started off with bankroll of $500. The first night I let them hit, for $100, but I'd taken in about $300. Then the next night I didn't let anybody hit. I took it all in, and that's how I got started.

I bought me a building after that and opened a liquor store and tavern. Then I went into the jukebox business. I had three taverns, one on the South Side (called *Club Mississippi*), one on the West Side (*Subway Lounge*) and another in Argo (*The Palm Gardens*). I also had about 10 girls working for me. I'm ashamed of what I did then but it did give me some insights into how cruel men can be toward women.

Besides my bars I had a good bootlegging business. After two in the morning you couldn't sell—not legally. And before twelve on Sundays you couldn't sell. And that's when my business was good.

In the meantime I was teaching school. Can you imagine me running policy and teaching school? I was teaching physical education and history. And I was a good teacher. All the kids loved me.

And another thing, you don't get business mixed up with civil rights. You can't spend civil rights. You can spend business. The reason I was able to do anything was because I was never dependent upon white folks. The Lord saw to it that I got to be independent of white people. I depended upon my people for a living. Now I can work and fight with them and I can work and fight for them without any economic reprisals being brought against me.

But June, 1963, Evers said, he was operating clean. He still had the tavern business in Chicago and an apartment house at 62nd St. and Normal. The building had 24 units and supplied income for him and Medgar. Charles lived on the first floor.

Medgar was shot fatally on June 12, 1963, and Evers rushed back from Chicago to take up his brother's post as Field Secretary for the NAACP. The fingerprints of Byron de la Beckwith were on the suspected murder weapon, but the White Citizens' Council, ably helped by the law firm of Governor Ross Barnett, got their man off. As leader of the NAACP in Mississippi Charles Evers led boycotts of segregated businesses and voter registration drives in Mississippi. In 1964 he funded and helped found the Freedom Democratic Party to challenge the segregated Mississippi State Delegation to the Democratic National Convention in Atlantic City, a move that was to thrust him into even more national prominence.

Perhaps the most dramatic and dangerous period of Evers' career came in 1965, when he led economic boycotts against local white merchants in Natchez, Fayette, and other Mississippi towns.

Evers tells of the campaign and some of the background:

Medgar and I got active in the NAACP in the late '40's when it began organizing state-wide. We'd both graduated from college and Medgar had gone to Mount Bayou, a small all-Negro town in the Delta, to sell insurance. I went back into the Service during the Korean War and it was in those days that I married Nannie McGhee, a childhood sweetheart from Mount Olive.

In 1958 Daddy got sick over in Decatur, seriously sick. We rushed him to the white hospital in Union, but they wouldn't admit him to a room or a ward like white patients, they just stretched him out on a cot in the basement, all damp and dark and crawling with roaches and rats. I argued and pleaded with them to put him in a ward, but they wouldn't listen to me. With proper care he might have got better but down in the basement he just wasted away and died. I kicked off a black voter registration campaign in Philadelphia, Mississippi, and I was elected voter-registration chairman for the Negroes of Mississippi. I pressed Medgar to be the first Negro to be enrolled at Ole Miss and in early 1954 he applied for admission. The board of higher education rejected the application but he had become an important symbol to Mississippi blacks; he was appointed state field secretary for the NAACP, which was preparing a big push in Mississippi after the Supreme Court's school desegregation ruling.

I was the first black disc jockey in Mississippi, on station WHOC, and I had a loyal audience. I'd always urge black folks over the air to go out and pay their poll tax and register to vote. I was also on my way to becoming a successful businessman with a healthy bank balance. Some whites started out to ruin me financially and they succeeded. I had several businesses at this time, a colored cab company, a burial-insurance business, as well as running my uncle's funeral parlor. I also ran a small hotel with a cafe which gave local black folks the first chance in their life to have a Coke or a milk shake while sitting down. But they [whites] pressured the owner of my hotel not to renew my lease, and they arranged it so I couldn't renew my cab license. They would run their cars into the side of my cabs or the hearse and sue. Finally they got a judgment of $5,000 against me and I just couldn't raise the money to pay it. So they took all my possessions. That was when I went to Chicago. It was 1956 and I stayed in Chicago until 1963 to make some money for Medgar. I came back in 1963 when he was killed. I took over Medgar's job as Field Secretary for the NAACP. . . . Until 1965 everything in Mississippi was segregated and blacks couldn't go into any of the public places. We made up our minds after the Civil Rights Bill was passed that we were going to desegregate all public accommodations. In May, 1965, we went into Natchez and desegregated all the hotels there. There were about 20 of us in Natchez and 300 rednecks. We were sitting in the Eola Hotel, trying to eat. We weren't hungry but we were sitting in there and they were outside with knives and guns, just pecking on the windows saying, "We're going to get you. We're going to get you when you come out." When we came out of the hotel all of the Klansmen met us at the door, but they began to back up as we walked out—and one thing about a racist is that if you look him in the eye and keep walking, he loses his courage. I was scared to death but they didn't know it. One of the burly white racists had a shotgun and another one was coming toward me with a knife about a foot long saying, "I'm gonna kill this sonofabitch." I was gonna grab him if he tried to knife me. But two white newspaper reporters stepped between us. They were fearless. They had guts. This saved me from getting cut because if the Kluxers had cut me every Negro would have turned that town inside out and a lot of people would have gotten killed right there.

Then one night in Natchez, at a mass meeting, an FBI agent came to me and said, "Mr. Evers, I'd advise you not to go out that door tonight because they're going to kill you." I said, "Who are you to tell me they're going to come here to kill me! Can't you stop them?" "No, our job is not to make arrests before but afterwards."

"Well, I don't need you around here. Get the hell out of my face. I don't need anybody telling me somebody's going to kill me. Well, if they're going to kill me they got a chance." And I just walked on out the door. The guards and troopers were out there and nothing happened.

It was in Natchez that we made our greatest score in the economic and political field when we desegregated 20 plus stores at one time. They hired black clerks, they hired black policemen—the ones we chose. This is what the dollar can do, this is what the boycott can do. We boycotted those stores till they saw the light. If black people in this country would just realize the importance of sticking together. This is how we get what we get in Mississippi. We had our protective squad. We had all our own guns. We didn't go around bragging about it, but we were ready to enforce those boycotts, to die if necessary. And they knew we were ready. We'd do it all over.

By 1967, under Evers' leadership, blacks gained electoral majority in five rural counties south of Jackson, resulting in the election of several Negroes to local offices. Evers tried and failed to win election to Congress in 1968. He won a plurality in the primary but lost in the runoff. In August of 1968 Evers became Democratic National Committeeman from Mississippi and became mayor of Fayette a year later.

When I got elected mayor of Fayette the threats started pouring in. The Kluxers would call me on my unlisted number and tell me there was gonna be one smartass nigger less around soon. But those threats don't really amount to much as long as they stay on the phone or stick to those anonymous letters. When you gotta watch out is when they stop talking and start shooting.

You know I still have bodyguards. Every black man's life is in danger in Mississippi. We go cheap down here—you learn to drink that in with your mama's milk. My life ain't worth a plugged nickel. I know that. I know they can gun me down in the back any time, just like they did Medgar. But that's not gonna stop me. Don't get me wrong. It's not that I'm so brave or nothing like that, but I seen so much death around me it's just stopped scaring me.

The bodyguards don't really make a difference. If they really want to get you they'll get you. Look how they got Bobby [Kennedy]. He was a few feet away from me, with all his bodyguards around, and it still didn't do any good. But I've always believed—and Medgar felt the same way—that what counts isn't how many years you live, or the way you die, but what you do while you're here. And you can't make any contribution if you live in fear.

People ask if the FBI has been active in investigating threats against my life and the answer is no. It was in Natchez, you remember, when an FBI man came to me in a church where we were holding a meeting and told me not to go out the door or I would be killed. Then after Medgar was killed and the FBI came to question me as if I might have done it—and I was in Chicago at the time. I ordered them out of my office.

The way it goes down here has always been murder followed by whitewash, followed by more murder. And after a while white folks get the idea it's no crime killing black folks, 'cause they always get away with it. I don't get as riled up at the thought of my own death as some of my friends up North do. When death has been walking right behind you since you were a baby you get used to it. I grew up with death. He's almost one of the family by now.

But since I was elected mayor the difference in Fayette is like the difference between night and day. Ten years ago if a black man was driving through Fayette he prayed that his car would not break down. Now people walk the street unafraid. You wouldn't even recognize Fayette today. And the old days when almost everybody was on the relief have gone. You know the ITT plant here brings in a monthly payroll of $40,000. But it's not just the economic benefits that are so important. It's the whole atmosphere of the town. For the first time black folks feel they have a community of their own that they can take pride in building and improving. We're getting black youngsters involved in community work and it is giving them a new sense of self-respect. Black people hold their heads high in Fayette today. But I won't have no truck with separatism, Fayette is a genuinely biracial town where blacks and whites can live together in harmony and mutual respect. It is vital we succeed because Fayette is a testing ground, a test to see if reason and tolerance can win out over the extremists on both sides.

If we can lick this racism in Fayette we can lick it in all of Mississippi, and if we can do that we can lick it in the nation. But if we fail in Fayette then a lot more than Fayette will be lost.

ITT has been a big part of our success.

The ITT participation in the Fayette Experiment is only a small part of its program of helping others. Through this program of corporate responsiveness it has carried out projects that range from school lunch programs in Louisiana to helping the blind in Zambia.

In a program devoted to equal opportunity, ITT has provided jobs and skills for more than 8,000 disadvantaged persons since inception of a program sponsored by the National Alliance of Businessmen and its Job Opportunities in the Business Sector.

It has participated in the NAB summer Youth Program with summer employment for almost 2,000 needy students.

A $200,000 grant to Rutgers University in New Jersey helped fund a Minority Enterprise Small Business Investment Company (MESBIC) to help would-be entrepreneurs from minority groups, and more than 40 New Jersey entrepreneurs have successfully entered business through this program.

"ITT shows evidence of a corporation that's really doing something," Mayor Kenneth Gibson of Newark, N.J., said. "ITT shows action and not just rhetoric."

ITT has shown its interest in young people. It has sponsored basketball tournaments in Harlem and Milwaukee, a safety education program, Little League baseball, and hot school lunches.

There have been programs to protect the environment, to bring European ballet to Brooklyn, to teach teachers how to deal with drug abuse, programs to help the American Indians, and programs to help the physically handicapped in such far away places as Australia and Zambia.

LLOYD L. BYARS

Lloyd L. Byars is an Associate Professor of Management in the School of Business Administration and a member of the Urban Life faculty at Georgia State University. He has published numerous articles in business and professional journals. Some of these journals include: *The Training and Development Journal, Advanced Management Journal,* and the *Journal of Systems Management.* His book, *The Management of Enterprise,* was published by the Macmillan Company in 1973.

Before joining the faculty of Georgia State, Byars worked as a marketing representative in the Data Processing Division of the IBM Corporation. He made the IBM One Hundred Per Cent Club during both of his years as a quota salesman and also received a Regional Manager's Award for outstanding marketing performance.

Byars has taught classes in Management Policy, Labor Relations, Personnel Administration, Production Management, Quantitative Methods, and General Management. He has served as a consultant and trainer to over 30 private and governmental organizations. Some of these organizations include the Department of Health, Education, and Welfare; the United States Civil Service Commission; the

MICHAEL H. MESCON

Michael H. Mescon is Regents' Professor of Human Relations and Chairman, Department of Management, School of Business Administration, Georgia State University. He has held, since its inception, this nation's first Chair of Private Enterprise.

Mescon is the author of over 60 articles and co-author or co-editor of the books *Organization and Enterprise* (Nexus, 1964), *The Management of Enterprise* (Macmillan, 1973) and two volumes of *Man and the Future of Organizations* (Georgia State University, 1972, 1973). He writes a monthly management column in several trade publications.

Mescon was honored by the American Economic Foundation (1964) for work in economic education, received the Freedoms Foundation George Washington Honor Medal Award (1968), and was awarded a special citation by the Joint Council on Economic Education (1972).

Mescon was guest lecturer at Hebrew University and the University of Tel Aviv, Israel. He inaugurated the Tandy Distinguished Lecture Series at Texas Christian University. He delivers about 125 lectures a year to various academic, professional, and civic

State of Georgia, including the Department of Health and the State Auditor's Office; the City of Atlanta; Fulton National Bank; General Cinema Corporation; Manpower Incorporated; and others. He is an arbitrator of labor-management grievances and is certified by the Federal Mediation and Conciliation Service and the American Arbitration Association.

Byars holds a Bachelor of Electrical Engineering degree and a Master of Science degree in Industrial Management from Georgia Institute of Technology. He holds a Ph.D. degree in Business Administration from Georgia State University.

He is a member of the following professional organizations: Academy of Management, American Management Association, Society for the Advancement of Management, Industrial Relations Research Association, and Southern Management Association.

groups. Active in community affairs, Mescon has served in consulting, training, and lecturing capacities for over 100 organizations representing business, academia, finance, and government. Additionally, he has occupied both line and staff positions in industry and served as an enlisted man in the United States Army.

Chapter 10

The Seven Sins of Management[1]

LLOYD L. BYARS

MICHAEL H. MESCON

The managers of businesses, like those of every organization, perform successfully in some areas but not so proficiently in others. In this chapter are presented seven areas in which management generally has performed below what might turn out to be survival level. These areas are so basic to the private enterprise system that management failure in these areas might be called sins against private enterprise.

Performance in these areas is controllable, as is shown by the excellent accomplishment in each of them by any number of individual managers and by management groups in any number of specific enterprises. The fact that excellent performance is clearly possible makes failure even more reprehensible.

This chapter is focused on private enterprise, but the sins presented here are equally present in many non-profit enterprises, including governmental and military organizations.

There are many reasons why management may be remiss in these areas. Perhaps the most common reason is a failure to recognize the importance of the problems these areas reflect. Whatever the reason for failure, any manager who does not give positive thought to and take effective action in these areas is not making his proper contribution to the vitality of his organization.

---

[1]Much of the material presented here is drawn from Chapter 21 of *The Management of Enterprise*, by Michael H. Mescon, William Rogers Hammond, Lloyd L. Byars, and Joseph R. Foerst, Jr., New York, Macmillan Company, 1973.

THE POOR TREATMENT OF PROFIT

Profit is both a major and an acceptable goal of a business organization. Current literature in management and related areas reflects a tendency by many to treat profit as if it were either amoral or immoral. Many leading entrepreneurs, industrialists, and administrators, who apparently have developed a skewed sensitivity to the concept of social responsibility, have echoed an equally untenable, unhealthy, and poor treatment of profit. Consider Charles Reich's statement, for instance:

> The impact of technology, market, and capitalism is written on our landscape, our culture, our faces. Perhaps the landscape shows it most vividly. In all societies prior to the modern, no matter how diverse in other ways, there existed an essential harmony between the people and the land, a harmony in which nature was not violently altered or violated. Modern society makes war on nature. A competitive market uses nature as a commodity to be exploited—turned into profit.[2]

This approach must inevitably weaken one of the basic tenets of private enterprise—the profit motive itself.

The basis for the solution to this condition has already been provided by writers who advocate both the realization of a profit *and* the satisfaction of individual and group needs. Numerous writers have provided excellent discussions on the positive treatment of profit. Roy Ash, former President of Litton Industries, describes profit as follows:

> The efficiency and the efficacy with which he [the businessman] performs this job is, in our system, measured by the profit which the businessman achieves for his enterprise. Profit is the measure of his responsiveness to the marketplace, as the customers which make it up go about determining the highest and best use of their resources.[3]

Peter Drucker describes profit this way:

> The argument that the capitalist should not be allowed to make profits is a popular one. But the real role of the capitalist is to be expendable. His role is to take risks and to take losses as a result. This role the private investor is much better equipped to discharge than the public one. We want privately owned business precisely because we want institutions that can go bankrupt and disappear. We want at least one institution that, from the beginning, is adapted to change, one institution that has to prove its right to survival again and again. This is what business is designed for, precisely because it is designed to make and to manage change.[4]

An example of one approach to the creation of a positive attitude

---

[2]Reich, Charles A.: *The Greening of America.* New York, Random House, 1970, p. 35.
[3]Learned, Edmund P., C. Roland Christensen, Kenneth R. Andrews, and William D. Guth: *Business Policy, Text and Cases* (Rev. Ed.). Homewood, Ill., Irwin, 1969, p. 850.
[4]Drucker, Peter F.: *The Age of Discontinuity.* New York, Harper & Row, 1969, p. 238.

toward profit was practiced at Westinghouse Electric and Alcoa. Both reported:

Managements at both companies firmly believe that employee understanding of the meaning of profit, and what it really measures, contributes much in other critical areas: easing the shock of a plant closing, making cost control programs really effective, gaining a necessary change in a labor contract.[5]

The private enterprise system must recognize the validity and necessity of the profit motive and must actively campaign to create a favorable image of profit and the profit motive. This can be done only by serious planning and extensive action on the part of management.

THE MYTH OF PROFESSIONAL MANAGEMENT

Management is not a profession at this time. The popular concept of a management elite is an economic fiction charged with assumptions, stereotypes, and misconceptions. Professional management too often merely means management by someone who is not also the owner of the enterprise.

Management, unlike the recognized professions of medicine, law, and others, has no singular and formal academic well from which all eventual practitioners *must* draw. One does not have to be accredited or certified by a recognized body to be a manager. Admission to the house of management is generally given by present managers. Many of these present managers have business backgrounds permeated by hunches, intuition, common sense, and experience, none of which can be effectively passed on to the newcomer. Many also have a sincere dislike for any entrance method that is standardized and control-oriented. Yet, all present professions are standardized and control-oriented. The result may be that the house of management is like a house of cards, which may not be able to sustain itself when the winds of social, political, and economic competition blow.

Nonprofessional management is self-defeating and masochistic in nature. It is unable of its own will and accord to perpetuate the type of business and institutional climate necessary to the maintenance of private enterprise.

INDIVIDUAL DIFFERENCES

The recognition of, and managerial action based upon, individual differences is vital to the survival of private enterprise. Apathy, disillusionment, and the establishment of antagonistic institutions are

---

[5]"Tell Employees About Profits," *Industry Week* (October 12, 1970), p. 29.

the natural consequence of ignoring this basic biological and social fact. Too many managers are finding the idea of recognition based upon merit both alien and unnecessary. It is a grave error to fail to understand that in a free economy individuals must be paid and rewarded on the basis of *merit*.

Only with strong managerial support can the concept of individual differences overcome the trend toward seniority as the determining factor in labor force movement and mobility. Where this concept is not recognized, mediocrity is rewarded, conformity becomes an end in itself, and an unhealthy situation for the organization comes into being.

The recognition of individual differences among managers is also important in a private enterprise system. If these differences are not recognized and individual merit is not rewarded, Gresham's law will start to operate, and the bad will drive out the good. If a manager looks around and sees less able men than himself doing the same job at approximately the same salary as his own, he will decide he is in the wrong place and will begin to look elsewhere. Thus:

> Promotions are the one visible, unmistakable sign of the corporation's standard of values, an irrevocable declaration of the qualities it prizes in its staff, a simultaneous warning and example to everyone who knows the nature of the job and the qualities of its new incumbent. Men who have worked diligently and successfully and then see those who have worked less diligently and less successfully promoted above them start to read the management want ads in the paper the following morning. Gresham's law operates more swiftly and inexorably through bad promotions than by any other agency.[6]

LACK OF TRAINING

The general lack of quality training in business, government, and industry is directly related to the management myth. Training is too often viewed by management as an organization extra, to be supported "if we can find the time" and to be dropped as the first step in the slightest retrenchment. So long as these views are widely held, private enterprise is in jeopardy. For example, a research study of personnel executives revealed the following results:

> The personnel executives in the survey reveal unawareness of facts related to the interview, job satisfaction and productivity, supervisory style, psychological stress, and other problems they must deal with.[7]

It is unrealistic, almost fantastic, to assume that the very difficult task of managing complex enterprises can be accomplished contin-

---

[6]Jay, Antony: *Management and Machiavelli*. New York, Holt, Rinehart and Winston, 1967, p. 178.

[7]Gannon, Martin J., and John P. Noon: "Management's Critical Deficiency," *Business Horizons, 14*:1, 49, 1971.

ually by untrained supervisors and managers. Peter Drucker explains the future of management training as follows:

> We have, in other words, a great deal to learn about management. Indeed the great age of management as a discipline is probably still ahead. But the "heroic age" in which the discipline was founded is behind us. It lay in the quarter-century before World War II. Then the basic thinking was being done by such men as the Frenchman Fayol, the Britishers Ian Hamilton and Urwick, and the American Alfred Sloan at General Motors, to name only a few of the pioneers. They made possible the great organizing feats of World War II in all combatant countries. Since then, in business and government as well as in the military, we have, by and large, only refined what was first learned in the twenties and thirties and first applied in the early forties.[8]

There are some in management with a seemingly intuitive and workable approach to the problems of getting things done through others. There are only a few of these, and it is unrealistic to hope that others will acquire these rare abilities by a kind of organizational osmosis. The only realistic solution is training.

The training function must have proper financial support. It must be staffed by persons who are properly trained themselves, and it must be known throughout the organization that top management is serious about training as a permanent and important function.

The training function must be objective-oriented, and the results of the training must be properly evaluated. Many training programs have no objectives at all. The adage, "training for training's sake," seems to be appropriate in these situations. On the other hand, programs with established objectives normally do not provide for the evaluation of results. If training departments are to provide valuable service in tomorrow's organizations, they must be able to evaluate and present the results of their work objectively. A valid training effort will enhance the probability of corporate survival. A sound approach to training by business will generally enhance the survival of private enterprise.

THE LEGALISTIC NATURE OF LABOR RELATIONS

A seemingly endless chain of conflict is an all too common characteristic of labor-management relations. This fact, along with the growing strength of the labor movement, is a significant commentary on management's ability to manage.

Management should realize, as the unions do, that unions are built and nurtured on management mistakes. One of these mistakes is management's use of an almost exclusively legalistic approach to labor relations. It is unrealistic to take a legalistic approach to what is essentially a marketing phenomenon.

The real competition between management and unions lies in an

---

[8]Drucker, *op. cit.*, pp. 198–199.

attempt of each group to convince the worker that the institution it represents can better satisfy the needs of individuals. A. A. Imberman gives the following description of why people join unions:

> The real motivating force toward joining a union is the feeling on the part of employees that they are not being treated fairly and decently. They base their feelings on such factors as: toilets are dirty; eating areas are dirty; parking lots are muddy; factory equipment is too old, faulty, or unsafe; the working areas are too hot or too cold; foremen are arbitrary and abusive; overtime or shorttime are distributed unfairly; incentive rates are considered unfair or unevenly distributed; the profit-sharing plan is misunderstood; wage or benefit differentials in the plant are biased; merit raises are late; seniority is often disregarded; new employees are hired to fill the best jobs; most of all, nobody in management listens to employees or cares what they think or feel about anything. They are treated apparently only as machine tenders or as adjuncts to the manufacturing process.[9]

Of course, management can only convince the workers that management can better satisfy the needs of individuals if, in fact, the company can better perform this function. Whether the company can or cannot is determined by management's total effectiveness.

The highly legalistic structure of contemporary labor relations is a superficial, after-the-fact attack on this problem area. Insofar as management is concerned it is often not an attack at all but a retreat or at best a rear-guard action.

Only a well-trained, professional management can successfully cope with the attrition and worsening of labor relations. The inability of nonprofessional management to recognize the real nature of this problem is the primary reason for its failure. The unwillingness of management to seek out and work with the causes of these problems may, in the end, remove even the treatment of their symptoms from management.

POOR COMMUNICATIONS

Numerous examples can be cited to indicate this sin. One of the humorous examples is indicated here:

> NO PANTS?
> NASHVILLE, TENN. (AP)—This notice was placed on the bulletin board of a Nashville insurance office: "Any of you show up wearing those hot pants will have to take 'em off the minute you walk through the front door."[10]

The authors are not sure whether the notice was serious or not. However, based on other examples of poor communication, the author of the notice may have been quite serious in his attempt to convey a company policy.

A somewhat more serious example also indicates the sin of poor

---

[9]Imberman, A. A.: "Why Do They Go Union?" *Industry Week* (November 23, 1970), p. 48.
[10]*Atlanta Journal,* April 28, 1971, p. 2.

communication. Over 1,000 employees of a company were questioned by Marsh & McLennan, Inc., a Chicago consulting firm, on their knowledge of the company benefit program. The results were as follows:

Half knew so little about the benefit program — or cared so little about it — that they didn't even bother to reply.

Of those who did answer, only about six in ten felt they understood the company's medical, profit-sharing, disability, life insurance, and retirement benefits.

In fact, far fewer really did.

For example, only 25 per cent of those who responded actually knew what surgical benefits they were entitled to under the company's basic health plan. Only 40 per cent knew how much group life insurance they could get.[11]

In addition, the results of recent attempts to correlate the amount of money spent on "selling" private enterprise with the effectiveness of these selling efforts are not surprising in that the effect of the money spent appears to be either negligible or negative. The communicative efforts of management in this area too often are directed toward condemnation rather than enlightenment. In order to sell the concept of private enterprise, the idea must first be communicated by one who is fully aware of its meaning.

Management, which must provide leadership in these attempts, has relied too much on pamphlets, brochures, house organs, and bulletin boards. Private enterprise, like any other idea, can best be communicated face-to-face by people who are not only dedicated but knowledgeable as well. Within the company and the community, where efforts of this sort must start, it is well to remember the truth of the trite old statement — that actions speak louder than words. Many good words lose their effect in the face of the act, for example, management's accepting — or even worse initiating — a wage system that ignores individual differences.

THE LOWLY STATUS OF WORK

The status of work, after several centuries of enjoying a very high level of esteem, has regressed almost to its nadir of the classical historical period. In the city of Rome during the Empire, work was considered acceptable for two classes of people: foreigners and slaves. Commerce and business stood in such low regard at that time that it probably was not by chance that Mercury, the god of thieves, was also god of commerce. Today statements such as the following appear to describe the working environment:

Work and living have become more and more pointless and empty. There is no lack of meaningful projects that cry out to be done, but our working days are used up in work that lacks meaning; making useless or harmful products,

---

[11]"Industry's Untold Multibillion-Dollar Story," *Nation's Business*, May, 1971, p. 62.

or servicing the bureaucratic structures. For most Americans, work is mindless, exhausting, boring, servile, and hateful, something to be endured while "life" is confined to "time off."[12]

In addition, the four-day work week fad is upon us. Is reducing the work week the answer? The authors of this chapter feel that the answer to this question is a resounding *no.*

Many things, most of them inevitable, have diminished the content and have lowered the dignity of work. It is not necessary to examine the consequences of automatic mass production to realize that the worker in modern industry lacks social status and recognition as an individual. This denial of individuality is really the essence of the new approach. In modern industry the worker is sometimes viewed only as a sloppily designed machine, and the process by which this machine is made to function effectively is the relatively new science, "human engineering." This new technique requires the standardization and interchangeability of the units of the labor force. It demands labor without status, function, or individuality. Management must take more affirmative and comprehensive action to offset, as much as possible, this negative side effect of progress. A man who feels that he is important, which he can do only if he feels that his job is necessary and of some significance in the organization, will not view work merely as an unpleasant interlude between weekends.

The present low regard for work is not only harmful to virtually every business enterprise, but it is also harmful to pure governmental operations as well.

A FINAL COMMENT

Some may feel that the accusations in this chapter seem too severe. Certainly, many groups other than management have had a part, for example, in bringing profit into question and in lowering the status of work. But it is management's responsibility to offset, not contribute to, these detrimental trends and events.

Private enterprise is a strong and vigorous reality. It is so strong and so vigorous that it can withstand, as it has in the past, much abuse from within and without, from its enemies and, indeed, from its friends. Yet, it must be assumed that there are limits beyond which abuse, whatever its source and nature, may wear or distort. Malfunctions in a system lead to attrition and modifications in the system; they may, but they do not *necessarily,* lead to its betterment.

The verbal philosophy of private enterprise must be overtly manifested in the behavior of businessmen, if private enterprise is to remain private. This philosophy must be reflected in the behavior of managers, if, in the end, there is anything to be managed.

---

[12]Reich, *op. cit.,* p. 17.

Chapter 11

Epilogue

The question of the legitimacy of social responsibility on the part of business is a moot one. Acting in a socially responsible fashion is an integral part of the executive's role. In actual fact, it is a matter of system survival.

The socially sensitive administrator fully comprehends that his business is but one segment of a greater societal framework. Yet, although it is but one segment, it is a highly visible one, and right or wrong, one whose basic motivations are constantly being questioned, challenged and scrutinized in a fashion that would completely debilitate lesser institutions.

Interestingly enough, even in the realm of politics, we seem to be more concerned with a candidate's investment portfolio than we are with his political philosophy. Apparently, once the profit ingredient is added, morality is thought to be lost. Not only is this belief ludicrous, but it also defies any attempt to secure substantive support except on an isolated basis.

In truth, corruption and immorality are in abundant supply. Business has not cornered the market. While some businessmen and their institutions behave in a less than responsible fashion, an identical indictment can be made about some physicians and their hospitals, some union leaders and their organizations, some clergymen and their religious institutions, some college presidents and their schools, and some governmental administrators and their agencies, to cite just a few.

That social irresponsibility is pretty well shared does not make it proper. Those of us who are concerned should wish a plague on all of their houses and then get busy, in a socially responsible way, to clean things up, beginning, of course, with our own individual areas of responsibility.

In essence, we need to move away from stereotypes and focus on specific behaviors. This is the mode of the truly enlightened person and is the basis for understanding and acceptance. Broad brush

159

condemnation is the style and strategy of the dictator and despot and has been since the beginning of time.

Today, social responsibility is almost an obligation that we inherit in a world searching for peace or at least peaceable accommodation. The rejection of this socially transmitted birthright can only lead to more of what we say we don't want or need.

Actually, social awareness as a requisite for business operation is not of recent vintage. Robert Owen, an early 19th century textile manufacturer, felt a strong sense of concern for his employees and fully believed that he would profit more if his people, i.e., his employees, profited more. By recognizing individual productivity and rewarding it, both did profit.

F. W. Taylor, who is often called the father of scientific management, was of the opinion that management's primary purpose was to secure maximum prosperity for both the employer and the employee.

It would appear that both Owen and Taylor had an exquisite sense of social responsibility, directed primarily toward a company's staff—and who is to say that this emphasis is misplaced? The fact that good employee relations is good business certainly does not make such views less noble or socially significant, although to "professional injustice collectors" such concern by the businessman is always deviously motivated and entirely self-serving. To them, the purging of profit from the system represents the only legitimate path to salvation. To the professional injustice collector, the socially responsible businessman is the one who first gets frightened. Chances are, exposure to reality won't alter his conclusions.

However, it is our expectation that The Other Side of Profit will add at least one other dimension, on an individual firm basis, to what some businesses are doing to make this world a better one.